HOW TO PAY LESS ...

AND KEEP MORE FOR

ROB CARRICK

YOURSELF

THE ESSENTIAL
CONSUMER GUIDE
TO CANADIAN BANKING
AND INVESTING

DOUBLEDAY CANADA

LIBRARY AND ARCHIVES CANADA CATALOGUING IN PUBLICATION

Carrick, Rob, 1962–
   How to pay less and keep more for yourself : the essential consumer guide to Canadian banking and investing / Rob Carrick.

ISBN-13: 978-0-385-66276-5
ISBN-10: 0-385-66276-9

   1. Finance, Personal—Canada. 2. Banks and banking—Canada.
3. Investments—Canada. 4. Consumer education—Canada. I. Title.

HG179.C29 2006   332.02400971   C2006-904757-X

Printed and bound in Canada

Published in Canada by
Doubleday Canada, a division of
Random House of Canada Limited

Visit Random House of Canada Limited's website: www.randomhouse.ca

TRANS   10   9   8   7   6   5   4   3   2   1

To Theresa, Will, and Jamie

Your love and support are what it's all about.

CONTENTS

HOW TO PAY LESS
AND KEEP MORE FOR
YOURSELF

BANKS, MUTUAL FUND COMPANIES, AND INVESTMENT dealers are among the most successful corporations in Canada, and they have you to thank for it. Yes, it's your hard-earned money that made these companies what they are today. Add up all the fees you pay to your bank, fund companies, and financial adviser and then combine them with the money paid by other clients. The resulting flow of multi-billions in annual revenue makes companies in the financial sector among the richest in Canada.

This calls to mind an often-told story about a self-important investment adviser who was visiting a marina with a friend and showing off the fancy boats that he and some of his fellow advisers owned. "Nice," said the friend, "but where are all the clients' boats?" Let's be fair—some people do get rich with the help of the financial services industry, and just maybe they get to float their boats with the big guys. As for the rest of us—well, let's just say there's a monetary imbalance between what the Bay Street brigade is pulling in and what's left over for us. You'll see it in those bank accounts that pay zero interest while raining down fees, in mutual funds that never seem to make as much money for you as they do for the companies that run them, and in the services of investment advisers who worry less about your financial progress than their own. The whole idea behind the financial services industry is to make money by helping you make and manage your money. It's a totally valid model, but not always a fair one in real life.

This book is your road map out of the dysfunctional relationship that too many Canadians have with the financial industry. You need banks, fund companies, and advisers as much as they need you, so I'm not advising you to stuff money in your mattress or adopt any similarly crazy strategy. Rather, the point is to give you the information you need to bring equality to your relationships with providers of financial services. In other words, give you the tools to get the most from banks and other financial services companies while paying the least.

Years ago, the idea of questioning the cost and quality of the products you bought from a bank, broker, or fund company would have seemed absurd to the vast majority of people. I remember going to the bank for my first mortgage in 1993, and waiting to be told what interest rate the bank would deign to offer. I also recall a meeting with a broker a couple of years later at which I was told exactly what I would be investing in and exactly how much it was going to cost. In both cases, I didn't know enough to question what I was told. Even if I had known, it would have been explained to me—oh so politely—that if I didn't like the deal, I could shove off.

Today, you don't get quite the same treatment. The Internet provides a lot of information on rates and fees, so most financial service providers can't treat you like a complete ignoramus (a partial ignoramus, yes). Also, competition is so intense between banks, fund companies, and advisory firms that everyone now recognizes the need to provide a certain degree of forthrightness and respect. Still, we have not yet arrived at a level playing field, to use a cliché favoured by those on Bay Street. While there are all kinds of great deals out there in banking products, mortgages, funds, and so on, you often have to know about them to take advantage. Example: Whereas it used to be a triumph to get a full percentage point knocked off your mortgage, today it's often possible to get an even bigger discount. Don't expect your banker to volunteer this information, though. Instead, you have to ask.

This book tells you how to ask for better terms. And if you ask and still don't get what you want, it tells you where to go for a better deal. Here we arrive at one of the current key trends in financial services. While all of the big companies want to have a relationship with you—in other words, sell you lots and lots of stuff—the truly savvy individual has many relationships with many companies. I'm a good example. I have my chequing accounts with one bank, my savings account with another, my mortgage with yet another, and my main credit card with still another. Yes, it might simplify life to aggregate all of these prod-ucts with one institution, but the net result would be to make that single institution richer at my own expense. That's the opposite of what this book's all about.

So, who am I to tell you how to deal with the financial industry? Let's just say this book has been more than eight years in the making, during which time I have written a regu-lar column on personal finance for *The Globe and Mail*,

Canada's national newspaper. I've spoken to hundreds of executives at banks, fund companies, brokerages, and financial advisory firms over the years, so I know how their world turns. At the same time, I have received (and, almost always, answered) tens of thousands of emails from readers asking questions and relating their experiences. I'm the guy in the middle, and I know both sides of the story.

HOW MUCH CAN I SAVE, AND HOW MUCH MORE CAN I MAKE?

A lot. Want specifics? Let's say you pull the money you're saving for a vacation out of a regular savings account and move it to a high-interest savings account offering, say, 3 percent. The difference between this and the microscopic or non-existent interest paid by your bank could easily be worth $100. A better deal on your mortgage and line of credit should save you a few hundred dollars a year in interest, and lower-cost mutual funds could pad your gains by even more. Let's do a quick rundown to give you the big picture.

Your Savings Account

Current profile: You have $3000 in a bank savings account that earns 0.1 percent annually. *Total interest earned per year: $3*

After you read this book: You have $3000 in a high-interest savings account earning 3 percent annually. *Total interest earned per year:* $90

Net gain: $87

Your Chequing Account

Current profile: You spend $15 per month in bank service and account fees. *Total cost per year:* $180

After you read this book: You find a cheaper package, at $8 per month, that better suits your style of banking. *Total cost per year:* $96

Net gain: $84

Your Mortgage

Current profile: You are about to sign up for a five-year $200,000 mortgage at a rate of 5 percent (twenty-five-year amortization), which your bank tells you is the best rate it can offer. *Payments:* $582 (accelerated biweekly, which means every two weeks), or $15,132 per year.

After you read this book: You have a $200,000 mortgage at a rate of 4.5 percent. *Payments:* $553, or $14,378 per year.

Net savings: $754

Your Line of Credit

Current profile: You take out a $10,000 unsecured credit line at an interest rate of 7 percent. *Cost:* $700 per year, assuming you pay only the interest.

After you read this book: You have a $10,000 home-equity line of credit at an interest rate of 5 percent. *Cost:* $500 per year, assuming you pay only the interest.

Net savings: $200

Your Investments

Current profile: You have a $100,000 portfolio of mutual funds with built-in fees averaging 2.8 percent annually. *Cost:* Fees reduce your returns by $2800 over a year.

After you read this book: You have a $100,000 portfolio of mutual funds with built-in fees averaging 2 percent annually. *Cost:* Fees reduce your returns by $2000 over a year.

Net gain: $800

TOTAL FINANCIAL BENEFIT OVER ONE YEAR:	**$1925**
LONG-TERM BENEFIT (FIFTY YEARS):	**$96,250**

Let's be straight about these numbers. They're meant as a rough estimate of how much you can save/gain if you're not following any of the advice in the book already. You might realize a smaller net benefit in real life, or it may be greater. The point is that by changing the way you bank and invest, you can realize tangible benefits that can easily take tens of thousands out of the coffers of banks, fund companies, and investment dealers and put them directly into your pocket.

ONE

CREATE YOUR OWN FINANCIAL PROFILE

GO BACK ABOUT TEN OR TWENTY YEARS AND ALMOST everyone conducted their financial affairs in the same way. Most transactions required a trip to the bank to visit a teller. For more complicated transactions, you'd telephone the bank for an appointment with the branch manager or perhaps a lower-tier flunky. Some of us still bank that way, but most have discovered that technology has completely changed our relationship with banks and other financial services providers.

It's now possible to conduct about 97.5 percent of all financial dealings on the Internet using bank and brokerage websites and email. Some people—I'm one of them—will exploit every opportunity to bank or invest online, while others use the Internet in a limited way, maybe to comparison shop, to monitor their bank balances, and perhaps to pay bills and transfer money from one account to another. Others either feel uncomfortable using the computer technology that makes Internet banking accessible to individuals, or mistrust it because of privacy concerns. For them, it's face-to-face contact or nothing.

Which way is best? I have an opinion, but I'll spare you, because one of the first rules of effective management of your financial affairs is to find the way to transact business that makes you feel most comfortable. I figure there are three ways to bank and invest, and have written this book so that people who fall into each group will find useful information. You love the Internet and would rather undergo a colonoscopy than visit a bank branch? I'm with you, buddy. You despise the Internet as an agent of technological imperialism and demand face-to-face contact when doing business? I'm with you, too, though I think you need to lighten up a bit. The point is, this book addresses all needs. Simply use the questionnaire below to determine your financial profile, and then refer to your profile in each of the six remaining chapters for quick briefings tailored to your needs. Before you complete the questionnaire, let's look quickly at the three profiles.

Profile One: **Online Warriors**
Whenever possible, you use nothing but the Internet and other forms of electronic banking and investing.

Profile Two: **Half and Halfers**
You're comfortable using the Internet for research and basic banking, but not comfortable making large transactions online.

Profile Three: **Traditionalists**
You rarely, if ever, use the Internet, and prefer to conduct financial business face to face.

Not sure where you fit in? Consider each of the ten questions below and circle the answer that seems most comfortable to you.

1. I need some cash. My preferred way of getting it would be to:

A—Stop by my local branch and make a withdrawal through a teller.

B—Find a bank machine operated by my own bank.

C—Use the nearest bank machine, fees be damned.

2. I have a stack of bills to pay. My preferred way of paying them would be to:

A—Use the mail or stop by my bank and pay them through a teller.

B—Use a bank machine.

C—Pay online.

3. I need to move some money around between my savings and chequing accounts. To do this, I will:

A—Stop by my bank and have a teller move the money.

B—Use a bank machine or telephone banking.

C—Do it online.

4. I need a mortgage. To compare rates, I will:

A—Call or visit my bank and haggle for the best rate possible.

B—Call or visit a few different banks and maybe use the Internet to compare rates.

C—Use the Internet to survey the entire market, and possibly to apply for my mortgage.

5. I have a few purchases of $30 or less to make, and I don't want to put them on my credit card. Instead, I will:

A—Scramble to get some cash.

B—Use my cash until it runs out and then use Interac direct payment, better known as debit.

C—Use Interac for everything, even if I have the cash.

6. I am setting up a high-interest savings account with a financial institution other than my usual bank to save for a vacation. I will put money in the account by:

A—Mailing cheques.

B—Using the telephone to arrange electronic money transfers from one bank to another.

C—Using the website of the institution offering the high-interest account to set up regular electronic transfers.

7. I am interested in finding a credit card that offers travel rewards. To get information and apply for a card, I will:

A—Stop by a few different banks, and then ask for an application form when I find something of interest.

B—Use the Internet to get information from bank websites, and then stop by the bank that offers the card I like to get an application.

C—Use the Internet to comparison shop, and then apply for the card online.

8. I am setting up a registered retirement savings plan. My preferred way of running the account would be to:

A—Discuss all moves with my banker or investment adviser, either in person or on the phone, and receive monthly or quarterly account statements.

B—Discuss all moves with my banker or investment adviser—in person, on the phone, or on email—but also have online access so I can see how I'm doing whenever I want to.

C—I may want advice, but I also want the ability to make transactions online.

9. I have decided to invest in stocks using a discount broker to save money on commissions. I will do my trading:

A—Using the telephone.

B—Using a mix of the phone and my broker's website.

C—Using my broker's website only, thanks.

10. The amount of flexibility I want for my banking and investing is:

A—Low, in that I'm happy to conduct business during regular business hours.

B—Moderate, in that I would like the ability to look at my accounts day or night, should the need arise.

C—High, in that I want to be able to view my accounts and make transactions whenever I want.

Scoring

Once you have answered each question, total the number of times you chose answers A, B, and C.

- If you answered A five or more times, you're a **Traditionalist**.
- If your answers were more or less evenly split between A, B, and C, or if you answered B five or more times, you're a **Half and Halfer**.
- If you answered C five or more times, you're an **Online Warrior**.

A FEW MORE WORDS ABOUT YOUR FINANCIAL PROFILE

As was mentioned earlier, pick the profile that makes you feel most comfortable, not the one you think you ought to fit into. You may have heard a lot about how online banking can save you time and money, but you're not going to be able to exploit these benefits if using a computer causes you only stress and aggravation. Truth is, there are costs and benefits to each of the profiles. Let's take a closer look.

Profile One: Online Warriors

Benefits: You save time—you can bank or invest any time you want—and you often save money because of the lower-cost products available to online customers. You're also in a position to be well informed about your purchases because of the vast amount of comparative financial information available online.
Costs: Fees can mount up if you make too many electronic banking transactions, such as withdrawals at bank machines or debit. Also, you may not have a personal relationship at your bank to fall back on.

Profile Two: Half and Halfers

Benefits: You reap the time-saving and research benefits of the Internet, but still likely have personal contacts at your bank, financial advice firm, or investment dealer.
Costs: You may not save as much money as you could if you avoid making some transactions online.

Profile Three: Traditionalists

Benefits: You should be able to keep your service fees under control because you aren't running around racking up debits at stores and withdrawing money from bank machines, and you'll certainly know the people at your bank.

Costs: You'll spend a lot of time in bank lines, plus pay extra in some cases for financial transactions. If you don't use the Internet at all, you'll also have to work a lot harder to get the information you need to make sound financial decisions.

Conclusion: No matter what your financial profile, in this book you'll find ways to save money on financial products and get better service. It may seem at times like the best opportunities are reserved for Online Warriors and Half and Halfers, and this is certainly true in some cases. But Traditionalists shouldn't be discouraged. Even if you prefer to conduct your financial affairs the old-fashioned way, there are still ways to navigate the system more effectively. Traditionalists also have the most to gain from this book, potentially speaking. Even a limited foray into researching financial products online—mortgages are a perfect example—can reap thousands of dollars in savings.

By all means, try stretching yourself to manage your finances online, but always remember that the key to managing your financial affairs effectively is comfort. Saving money at the cost of extra stress and aggravation is a true false economy.

TWO

BANKING

Background briefing: A bank's idea of the perfect relationship with a customer is to have him or her sign up for a chequing account, a savings account, and a mortgage. From there, the bank might try to expand its role to include credit cards and lines of credit, mutual funds, guaranteed investment certificates, registered retirement savings plans, financial planning, and investment advice. All banks offer these services, but no single bank provides the best in service for the least in fees in all of these product categories.

There are two ways to deal with this reality: you can parcel out your bank accounts, mortgages, mutual funds, and so on to the best player in each area, or you can pick a "home bank" as a base of operations and farm out other products or services as necessary. The latter approach is the best one for most people, partly because it saves time but also because everyone needs to have a strong relationship with a bank—any bank—so he or she can pick up the telephone or send an email and have someone at that institution quickly help him or her out of a jam.

Another advantage of having a home bank is negotiating leverage. If you've got multiple lines of business with a bank, it's easier to get more advantageous terms in future dealings.

Your home bank will probably be the bank you've dealt with the longest, maybe because it had a branch near your childhood home, near your first serious job, or near that apartment you rented after you first moved out on your own. Maybe you feel a sense of nostalgia or familiarity when you see that bank's logo. Maybe they granted you your first loan, and maybe you sort of feel as if you grew up with them. Whatever your ties, it's time to reassess and make your bank work for each and every piece of business you give it.

FIRST THINGS FIRST:

THE WONDERS OF THE INTERNET AND ONLINE BANKING

The proportion of Canadians who regularly use online banking—that is, who make virtually all transactions other than deposits and withdrawals on their bank's website—seems to have stagnated in recent years at around one in three. This, to me, is a mystery. With life as busy as it is, and with computers as ubiquitous as they are, why would anyone not use online banking for at least some financial management?

Here are some benefits of banking online that speak to keeping your bank's mitts off your money as much as possible:

- Cheaper account and service fees in some cases.
- Easy transfers between chequing and savings accounts, and often between different financial institutions, so you can earn higher interest whenever possible.
- Access to your balances at any time so you can tell whether

cheques have cleared, whether you're overdrawn, whether automatic deposits and withdrawals have been made, and so on. By checking balances online, you'll avoid costly overdrafts.

- Greater ability to scrutinize your day-to-day banking, thereby enabling you to notice and eliminate wasteful habits that cause you to pay fees.
- No waiting in bank lineups (as the cliché goes, time is money).
- Instant access to information about interest rates and banking products on your financial institution's website.

So why do only a minority of people use online banking regularly? Some lack access to a computer, which is a good reason but not an insurmountable one if you consider that computers with Internet access are available in libraries, Internet cafés, and many workplaces. Some people are not comfortable moving sums of money around by clicking a computer mouse and relying on technology, which is fair enough until you consider that the banks themselves move money electronically all the time. And some people avoid online banking because of privacy and security threats, which are legitimate but not so worrisome to prevent you from making as many transactions on the Internet as you want.

This last point is worth reinforcing, because the Internet is sometimes portrayed as a cyberspace Wild West where scam artists troll for unwary victims. The reality is that online banking is safe. Yes, you can always dredge up a computer expert who believes it's possible for hackers—Internet delinquents, to the unfamiliar—to eyeball your account data or somehow steal your money. But worrying about stuff like this is akin to not going outside because of the risk that a meteorite will land on you. Here's why: all banks, credit unions, and other financial companies use a variety of effective measures to keep your data safe.

THE LAYER CAKE

Layered security is the term that financial services companies use to describe a series of measures that work to keep customer data private and to lock criminals out. These measures include:

- *Client user names and passwords,* which are meant to be kept secret by the client.
- *The "remember my card" feature on bank and brokerage websites.* This stores your user name or client card number (some numbers should be hidden) so that you don't have to type it in each time. Remembering your card number is a useful security feature because it offers a defence against a process known as key-logging, where someone remotely tracks the keys you type as you log into a website. Software that allows key-logging can be loaded onto your computer if you click on an attachment in an unknown email.
- *Sign-in protection,* which offers clients the option of registering any number of computers they use with their bank. If someone tries to access a client's account from a non-registered computer, the bank asks a pre-arranged question that only the client should be able to answer. Without a correct reply, access is denied.
- *128-bit encryption,* which means that your personal data are scrambled and unreadable while in transit between you and your bank.

Still not convinced about the merits of online banking? No worries—that's why this book includes advice for traditionalists who prefer face-to-face banking. Now, let's get down to business.

SAVINGS ACCOUNTS: AVOID THE BIG BANKS

Savings accounts are the easiest and, for many people, the most important financial vehicle for getting the most while paying the least. Who among us does not need a safe place to park money temporarily, to stash it away for emergencies, or to save up gradually for a house or other big purchase? Who among us has not at some point made the serious error of using a big-bank savings account for this purpose?

Big-bank savings accounts are like a penal colony for your money. If you've got a substantial amount of money sitting in one of these accounts, it's time to stage an escape. Consider one particular bank's savings account: you get a lusty rate of 0.05 percent on deposits up to $999.99, and the rate soars to 0.07 percent if your balance is between $1000 and $2999.99. Then things get tricky. For portions of your balance above $3000, you get the princely amount of 0.1 percent. Let's be clear here: the first $2999.99 is pegged at 0.07 percent and only the amount above that gets 0.1 percent. This method of setting interest rates is called tiering, and it's an insidious way to fool clients into thinking they're getting higher rates than they actually are. After all, it's human nature to look at the rate for a large deposit and assume you'll get that rate for the entire balance, not just a sliver of it. People are all the more likely to be fooled because even the best rates on big-bank savings accounts are so laughably minuscule that you're guaranteed to do a double take when reading them for the first time. *Could that really be 0.05 percent?* you'll ask yourself. Sadly, yes. Paying interest of 0.05 percent on funds that are then loaned out at 6 to 10 percent is the big-bank way of doing things. And just so you know how bad this rate really is, 0.05 percent is five cents of interest for every $100 per year. Call the Rolls-Royce dealer!

Some Big Banks Sort of Get It

While the Big Six banks are, as a rule, obtuse when it comes to savings accounts, a few have made a praiseworthy effort to deliver a proper offering in this product category. Examples are Bank of Nova Scotia and Bank of Montreal, where the MoneyMaster high-interest savings account and the Premium Rate savings account, respectively, pay rates that are vastly higher than the typical big-bank savings account. What's more, these rates are paid on your entire balance, with no tiering. Should you consider Scotiabank's MoneyMaster, BMO's Premium Rate account, or any other big-bank savings accounts, for that matter? Let's just say there are some very good alternatives out there, as we'll see.

HOW TO GET HIGH INTEREST ON THE LOWLY SAVINGS ACCOUNT

Add savings accounts to the list of ways in which the Dutch have enriched our lives here in Canada. The Amsterdam-based bank ING Group set up shop in Canada in 1997 as ING Direct, an operation built around a high-interest savings account that far exceeds the rates offered by the big Canadian banks and provides the additional advantage of zero fees. Today, ING

Direct has paid out more than $1.5 billion in interest to its Canadian customers, and is widely copied by other financial players, many of whom compete aggressively by offering rates one-quarter or one-half a percentage point higher than ING. Yet ING still has the quintessential product in this category, because it offers a competitive rate and easy access to your money.

What's the Big Deal?

As I am writing this book, ING offers a rate of 3 percent on its investment savings account. Okay, 3 percent is pitiful in the grand scheme of things. You could reasonably estimate that inflation will average something not too far from 3 percent over the long term, which would mean that ING's investment savings account offers a real return (after inflation) of zero. And yet, 3 percent is a darn good rate in the context of what is happening in the broader rate environment. One-year GICs—we're talking about locked-in money here, whereas high-interest accounts offer free access at any time—pay as little as 2.5 percent, while money market mutual funds have annual yields in the area of 2.7 percent. The bottom line here is that high-interest savings accounts commonly get you a premium of one-quarter to one-half a percentage point over other short-term parking spots for money, and they have a much bigger edge over big-bank savings accounts. If you're wondering how this is possible, remember that most high-interest account offerers are virtual operations that have no branches and do business electronically.

YOUR FINANCIAL PROFILE: HIGH-INTEREST ACCOUNTS

Online Warriors and Half and Halfers: Given that you're comfortable with the idea of online banking, you should have no trouble dealing with the banks, credit unions, and other financial companies that offer high-interest accounts.

Traditionalists: Don't worry, you can generally deal with these financial institutions by telephone, bank machine, and even mail, if you prefer depositing a cheque that way.

USING A HIGH-INTEREST ACCOUNT

If you deal with ING Direct or the vast majority of other providers of high-interest accounts, your best options for making deposits and withdrawals are to use either the telephone or the Internet for your transactions. Some banks also offer access to your money through automated bank machines. As well, you may be able to mail in cheques for deposit to your account.

Despite the obvious convenience, some people have a problem with moving money online or over the phone for a couple of reasons, the first being a lack of comfort with electronic banking. If this applies to you, I suggest you resolve to at least give it a try. My seventy-eight-year-old mother has only recently become computer-literate, and she's still leery of moving money around on the Internet. And yet, she's been an ING Direct customer for years, shifting her money back and forth from her regular big-bank chequing account over the telephone. She simply calls the toll-free number and speaks with one of ING's representatives. For security purposes, she provides both a client number and a personal identification number, known as a PIN. How much more basic can you get?

While the phone is great, the Internet is better. To get started, all you need to do is request a username and password from your bank and then send it a void cheque issued on your everyday bank chequing account. Any time you want to move your money, you log into your bank's website, indicate whether your want to move money in or out of your ING account and then specify the amount. One to three days later (no, money doesn't move instantly online), the transaction will be completed and the money moved. One complication is that the bank receiving your money will almost always put a "hold" on the funds for a period that can last five to seven days.

YOU CAN'T EVALUATE THE HIGH-INTEREST PLAYERS WITHOUT A SCORECARD

ING Direct is a fairly well known name these days, if for no other reason than those television commercials featuring a sour-looking fellow who tries to hector people into taking their savings away from the big banks and giving them to ING. But most other high-interest players aren't well known at all, so let's fix that.

Achieva Financial's Achieva Savings Account

Background: Achieva is a division of Winnipeg-based Cambrian Credit Union.

Moving money: Deposits can be made by mail, by regular automatic transfer from accounts at other financial institutions, or through bank machines in the Acculink credit union network. Withdrawals can be made at any bank machine.

Utility: This account offers chequing privileges, with one free cheque per month, plus online bill payment (cost: 50 cents) and a bank card that you can use for withdrawals (cost: 60 cents or $1, depending on the machine used) and debit transactions (cost: $1).

Deposit insurance: 100 percent of deposits guaranteed by the Credit Union Deposit Guarantee Corp. of Manitoba.

Verdict: Top rates and some regular banking services, but not ideal for people who will be transferring funds frequently between their regular chequing account and their high-interest account.

Info: www.achieva.mb.ca or 1–877–224–4382.

Altamira Investment Services' High-Interest CashPerformer

Background: Altamira, a mutual fund company, is a division of National Bank of Canada.

Moving money: Use the phone or the Internet to get money to or from a linked account at another bank.

Utility: Savings only.

Deposit insurance: Up to $100,000 in coverage through Canada Deposit Insurance Corp.

Verdict: Not the most convenient account, but has been making an effort to keep rates at the high end of the spectrum.

Info: www.altamira.com or 1–800–263–2824.

American Express Canada's Amex Investment Savings Account

Background: Amex is a global financial services company.

Moving money: Shift your money to a linked account at another bank on the Internet or by phone.

Utility: Strictly a savings account.

Deposit insurance: CDIC.

Verdict: Not especially competitive on rates.

Info: www.americanexpress.com/canada or 1–800–668–2639.

Bank of Montreal's Premium Rate Savings Account

Background: BMO is one of the few big banks to offer a high-interest account.

Moving money: Works in tandem with a regular BMO chequing account, which means you can easily transfer money between the two.

Utility: A basic savings account with deposits and withdrawals, but no bill payments or debit card purchases.

Deposit insurance: CDIC.

Verdict: Handy if you're a BMO client, but far from the best you can do in terms of rates.

Info: www.bmo.com or 1–800–363–9992.

Bank of Nova Scotia's MoneyMaster High-Interest Savings Account

Background: Scotiabank is the other big bank that offers a high-interest account.

Moving money: Designed as a companion to Scotiabank's chequing accounts, so you simply transfer money between the two.

Utility: Unlimited no-cost transfers using electronic banking; for all debits made directly from the MoneyMaster account, you pay $5.

Deposit insurance: CDIC.

Verdict: See BMO.

Info: www.scotiabank.com or 1–800–472–6842.

Citizens Bank of Canada's Ultimate Savings Account

Background: Citizens Bank of Canada is an online bank owned by the Vancouver City Savings Credit Union.

Moving money: Can be done electronically on the Citizens Bank website, to and from other financial institutions.

Utility: You get a bank card and four free withdrawals each month from bank machines in the Exchange network, which includes credit unions, HSBC Bank Canada, and National Bank of Canada.

Deposit insurance: CDIC.

Verdict: Not a huge rate premium over ING, but a good alternative.

Info: www.citizensbank.ca or 1–888–708–7800.

ICICI Bank Canada's HiSave Savings Account

Background: ICICI is a division of ICICI Bank Ltd. of Mumbai, India.

Moving money: Online transfers to and from accounts elsewhere; bank cards available on request for withdrawals.

Utility: A savings account only.

Deposit insurance: CDIC.

Verdict: Good rates, so-so utility.

Info: www.icicibank.ca or 1–888–424–2422.

ING Direct's Investment Savings Account

Background: ING Direct is a division of the Dutch-based financial services giant ING Group.

Moving money: Electronic funds transfer by Internet or phone.

Utility: A bank card allows you to make four bank machine withdrawals per month, with ING waiving any Interac network fees (you'll still likely pay up to $1.50 to the owner of the bank machine).

Deposit insurance: CDIC.

Verdict: Couldn't be easier to use, but lack of full-service banking (i.e., debit and chequing) and lower rates than some other accounts have cut into ING's overall appeal somewhat.

Info: www.ingdirect.ca or 1–800–464–3473.

Manulife Bank of Canada's Advantage Account

Background: Manulife Bank is part of Manulife Financial Corp.

Moving money: Electronic funds transfer using the Manulife Bank website, mail, deposit at Royal Bank of Canada branches, or bank machines in the Exchange network.

Utility: This account offers chequing, online bill payments, and a bank card that you can use for debit transactions or withdrawals at bank machines. Fees are 50 cents for debit transactions and bill payments and $1.25 for bank machine withdrawals.

Deposit insurance: CDIC.

Verdict: A formidable ING alternative from a name-brand financial player.

Info: www.manulifebank.ca or 1–877–765–2265.

Outlook Financial's High-Interest Savings Account

Background: Outlook is a division of Winnipeg's Assiniboine Credit Union.

Moving money: Transfers of money from another institution can be arranged by phone, by mail, or by using a website called Telpay.ca.

Utility: Online bill payments, chequing, and debit available, with one free transaction per month.

Deposit insurance: As a Manitoba credit union, Outlook's deposits are fully guaranteed.

Verdict: In exchange for top rates, you get a little less convenience in moving your money around.

Info: www.outlookfinancial.com or 1–877–958–7333.

President's Choice Financial's Interest Plus Savings Account

Background: PC Financial is an online bank operated by the supermarket chain Loblaw Cos. and Canadian Imperial Bank of Commerce.

Moving money: Online transfers between other PC Financial accounts, or other financial institutions.

Utility: No direct access to this account through bank machines or debit, so it's strictly a savings vehicle.

Deposit insurance: CDIC.

Verdict: Very competitive rate, but you need a $1,000 minimum to qualify. (Note: PC Financial's Interest First account has no minimum but offers a lower rate.)

Info: www.pcfinancial.ca or 1–888–872–4724.

Ubiquity Bank of Canada's Personal Client Account

Background: Ubiquity Bank is an online bank owned by B.C.-based Prospera Credit Union.

Moving money: Electronic funds transfer, or use Exchange network bank machines.

Utility: This is an all-purpose chequing account with a monthly fee of $7.50 that includes 35 transactions.

Deposit insurance: CDIC.

Verdict: Really a chequing account with a high interest rate that typically beats ING's.

Info: www.ubiquitybank.ca or 1–888–881–0188.

As you compare the various players, keep the following in mind: before ING arrived in Canada more than a decade ago, the big banks ruled the savings account market. Good riddance to that.

WHICH ACCOUNT TO CHOOSE?

The most obvious criterion for choosing a high-interest account is how high its rate is. Up-to-date rate comparisons are available on the website operated by financial data provider Cannex Financial Exchanges Ltd. (www.cannex.com). You'll find that several operators have positioned their rates to be somewhat higher than ING's, and that the online banks operated by credit unions tend to offer the highest rates. Accessibility is the next criterion. As the preceding comparison shows, some providers offer Internet and bank machine access while others require you to rely mostly on the telephone.

Fees are another issue. Generally, there should be no fee to move money to and from your account electronically, but you may encounter transaction fees if you make withdrawals through bank machines, write cheques, or use a client card for debit transactions. High-interest accounts are generally nothing more than holding pens for your money, but some do offer vestigial transaction capability at a price.

The final criterion for choosing a high-interest account is deposit insurance, which is worth discussing because it addresses the important issue of how safe your money is. Any serious financial institution in this country is either a member of Canada Deposit Insurance Corp., a federally run agency that protects deposits up to $100,000, or a provincial government–backed credit union deposit insurance entity that offers protection levels ranging from a low of $100,000 to unlimited coverage. Alternative banks such as Citizens Bank, PC Financial, ING, Amex, ICICI, and Manulife are all members of CDIC, while Achieva Financial and Outlook Financial are members of credit union deposit insurance plans through their parents.

Special note for clients of financial advisers: Many advisers now offer their clients high-interest accounts, and the rates can be quite competitive in some cases. Note that advisers may be paid a small ongoing fee for steering your money into a particular high-interest account. This money is paid by the institution offering the account, not by you, but it does raise questions about whether a particular high-interest account is being recommended because it has the best rates for you or the best compensation for the adviser. To be sure what you're getting, always ask your adviser to show you what other high-interest accounts are offering.

STRATEGIES FOR HIGH-INTEREST ACCOUNTS

Here's an idea I've used for years and highly recommend: every time you are paid, have some of your money transferred automatically to your high-interest account to help you save for the various big expenses that crop up throughout the year. For example, you could set up a property tax account and deposit some money into it every two weeks. If you've got a big annual car insurance bill, you could put away money every two weeks or every month for that as well. The advantage of saving this way is as follows.

SAVING THE HIGH-INTEREST WAY

To ensure that you'll have enough money on hand to pay the large expenses that crop up throughout the year, you will:

- Transfer $300 from your chequing account to your high-interest savings account once per month to save for property taxes.
- Transfer $150 to your high-interest account every two weeks to save for your car, house, and life insurance bills.
- Transfer $100 per month to your account to save for a family vacation.

Total deposits over 12 months:	$ 8700
Estimated total interest received at 3 percent on your steadily growing balance:	$ 141
Comparable interest from a big-bank savings account:	$ 24
Benefit to you:	**$ 171**

Note: Some financial institutions allow you to set up multiple accounts to which you can give informal nicknames. So, you could have a Property Tax account, an Insurance account and a Family Vacation account. Also, note that interest from any savings account is taxable.

CHEQUING ACCOUNTS: CHECKING OUT THE SAVINGS

Chequing accounts are an essential financial tool, and no reasonable person expects the banks to offer them for free. Except, well, you *can* get a free chequing account. It's quite easy, in fact. Many banks offer a free account if you maintain a minimum balance, and one financial institution, President's Choice Financial, offers free chequing accounts to anyone with a pulse. Want more information on this? You'll get it, but first you should know that free chequing accounts aren't the living end.

A more appropriate goal is to find a reasonably priced account, which means one for which you pay a fair price for the services you use. The way to do that is to examine your last few monthly bank statements, either on paper or online, and tally what you're actually paying in fees. Don't be naive enough to fall back on the fact that you've got a chequing account package from your bank with a set monthly fee. Many people have accounts like this, but end up paying a lot more for transactions not covered by their plans. For example, maybe you are allowed twenty-five withdrawals every month, but you've developed a liking for Interac debit transactions and find yourself making closer to forty withdrawals. If you're paying 50 cents apiece for the extra withdrawals, you'll fork over an extra $7.50 a month in fees. Your bank will love you for doing this, but haven't you got something better to do with this money?

YOUR FINANCIAL PROFILE: CHEQUING ACCOUNTS

Online Warriors: Chequing accounts are one area where it really pays—or, rather, saves—to be web-savvy. With their low-overhead, branchless operations, virtual online banks such as President's Choice Financial and Citizens Bank of Canada are able to offer everyday banking fees that are a far better deal than any big bank for most people.

Half and Halfers: Some of the most reasonably priced chequing accounts are aimed at people who do a modest amount of online banking, including bill payments and Interac direct payments, or debit.

Traditionalists: The big banks recognize that many of their customers prefer branch banking, and their account packages reflect this. Costs for these packages aren't especially cheap, unless you can restrict yourself to a small number of transactions per month.

Checking for Bargains

One of the latest and most welcome trends in banking is the "unlimited" chequing account, which permits you to make as many transactions as you need each month for a set fee. If you make a lot of withdrawals, Interac debits, and bill payments each month—let's say more than one to two dozen—then ask your bank if it has a product like this. Be sure to check what's included in the monthly fee—unlimited electronic transactions are typical, but some accounts may not include in-branch transactions. Also, overdraft protection and return of your cheques each month may or may not be included.

If you're not sure what type of account would be best, or if you just want to survey all the offerings, then take a look at the online Cost of Banking Guide offered by the Financial Consumer Agency of Canada (www.fcac.gc.ca), or the Financial Service Charges calculator offered on Industry Canada's Strategis website at www.strategis.ic.gc.ca (look under Strategis for Consumers). Provide these analytical tools with details on how you bank and they will compute the monthly cost at a variety of major banks and credit unions, including Bank of Montreal, Bank of Nova Scotia, Caisses Desjardins, Canadian Imperial Bank of Commerce, Citizens Bank of Canada, HSBC Bank Canada, Laurentian Bank, National Bank of Canada, President's Choice Financial, Royal Bank of Canada, TD Canada Trust, and VanCity, the country's largest credit union (and owner of Citizens Bank). If you're perchance wondering about ING Direct, it isn't included because it does not offer a transactional chequing account.

I ran three scenarios through the Strategis calculator: one for Online Warriors, one for Half and Halfers, and one for Traditionalists. To illustrate how costs can vary according to how you use your account, I arbitrarily created different banking habits for each of the three financial profiles. Also, for the first two profiles I assumed that the minimum balance in the account would be zero. For the Traditionalist profile, I assumed a minimum balance of $1000 would be maintained at all times (this can sometimes result in your fees being waived—read on). Another point worth noting is that the following comparison covers core banking only, not matters such as overdraft protection and the return of cancelled cheques to you every month.

These services often cost extra. One last point: this comparison is used strictly to provide an example of how fees vary and may not reflect the latest pricing.

Chequing Accounts for Online Warriors

This profile is based in part on the joint account my wife and I have. I've factored in:

- fifty-five Interac direct payments a month
- twenty-five withdrawals at the bank's ABMs
- six bill payments by Internet or by phone
- six account transfers by Internet or by phone
- three pre-authorized automatic debits
- five cheques
- one paycheque deposited each month

Cheapest option: PC Financial wins at the time of writing, thanks to its no-fee bank account.

Runners-up: VanCity's E-Package costs $7 per month, Citizens Bank's Chequing/Savings Account costs $8, National Bank's AccessPlus account costs $10.95, HSBC's Performance Package comes in at $11.50, CIBC's Unlimited Chequing Account comes in at $12.95, as does TD Canada Trust's Infinity Account.

Chequing Accounts for Half and Halfers

I estimated that someone in this category might typically use:

- seven cheques per month
- twenty Interac direct payments
- two in-branch withdrawals
- three pre-authorized debits
- six withdrawals at the bank's ABMs

- six bill payments (all by electronic means: ABM, phone, or online)
- three account transfers (electronic)
- one paycheque deposited each month

Cheapest option: According to the Strategis calculator, Scotiabank's Basic Banking package is the low-cost option at $8.50 per month at the time of writing.

Runners-up: BMO's Standard Plan at $11 per month, HSBC's Direct Banking Package at $11.25, Desjardins's Autonomous Plan at $11.50, and RBC's Royal Certified Service at $12.

Note: PC Financial and Citizens Bank were left out of this section of the comparison because they have no branches.

Chequing Accounts for Traditionalists

I estimated that this type of person might use:

- twelve cheques per month
- two bank machine withdrawals
- eight in-branch withdrawals
- three in-branch bill payments
- three in-branch account transfers
- three in-branch balance enquiries

Note: Monthly balance is kept at $1000 or more at all times.

Cheapest option: VanCity is cheapest with no fee, thanks to the $1000 minimum balance.

Runners-up: HSBC's Performance Activity Account at $4.05 per month, Laurentian Bank's DaybyDay Savings Plus Account at $6, Desjardins's Autonomous Plan at $8, and CIBC's Everyday Chequing Account at $9.

MAXIMUM SAVINGS FROM MINIMUM BALANCES

With a minimum of $1000 to $3000 in your account at all times throughout the month, Bank of Montreal, Citizens Bank, CIBC, TD Canada Trust, and VanCity are among the institutions that will waive some or all of your day-to-day transaction fees. I know that there are people out there who can manage the feat of maintaining a four-figure minimum balance in their accounts, because I hear from them every time I write a column complaining about chequing account fees. I have to confess, though, that I'm not like those people. Though I'm pretty good at managing my family's day-to-day finances, keeping a minimum balance of $1000 is an impossible dream. Keeping a chequing account with a positive balance—that's challenge enough.

Still, if you manage to keep your balance at four figures throughout the month, then the savings you'll enjoy can easily outweigh the interest you'd make if you invested that money even in a high-interest savings account. Keeping $1000 in an account to get $10 in fees waived every month for a year is a much better value than earning 2.5 percent interest on that same $1000. You'd save $120 in after-tax dollars with the $1000 in your account, compared with earning $25 in interest and having to pay tax on it.

If you're going to keep a minimum balance in your account, remember the rules. If your balance slips below the minimum, even for half a nanosecond, you lose your fee waiver. For that reason, it's probably a good idea to keep a little extra money in your account to help keep you above the minimum.

ATTENTION, SENIORS AND STUDENTS

Children and students of post-secondary institutions are like seniors in that almost every financial institution offers them a break on service fees. Don't fail to take advantage of these accounts, because they can be much cheaper than standard ones.

BANK MACHINES:
THE CRACK COCAINE OF THE BANKING BUSINESS

The most costly and ruinous addiction in banking today is the automated bank machine. ABMs most certainly are convenient. But they're also nasty beasts that can suck the life right out of your bank account if you're not strong enough to escape their clutches. Years ago, you could use an ABM operated by a bank you didn't have an account with and pay your home financial institution a fee of $1 to $1.50 to connect to the Interac banking network. Today, the bill is usually $3 if you're unfortunate enough to run out of money when your own bank's ABMs are nowhere in sight. What, $3 doesn't sound like a lot? If you're withdrawing $40 from your account, $3 represents a 7.5-percent surcharge. Use another bank's ABMs just once a week and you're looking at $156 in parasitic fees in one year.

YOUR FINANCIAL PROFILE: BANK MACHINES

Online Warriors and Half and Halfers: Banking online can save you money if you have the right account package, but darn few account packages shield you entirely from fees that apply when you use another bank's ABMs.

Traditionalists: Think you're immune to ABM fees if you never use a bank machine? Before you gloat, make sure you're not getting dinged for in-branch withdrawals at a teller.

Here's how the fees stack up when you use ABMs owned by other banks or by independent no-name operators. First, your own bank will generally levy a $1.50 network connection fee when you use another institution's ABM. On top of that, the owner of the bank machine will charge you in the area of $1.50, or more in rare cases, as a money-grabbing surcharge. You could end up paying even more than $3 per ABM visit if your bank account package has a withdrawal service charge. How can you stop this madness? Here are some options:

- Make large withdrawals when you're at your own bank's ABMs so you don't need to make repeat visits. I dislike carrying a roll of cash around, but I hate those service fees even more.
- Use the Interac direct payment system, commonly known as debit. Even if your bank account levies a fee on a debit payment, it's likely to be around 50 cents. One thing to watch out for is that some small stores have debit terminals

that charge a service fee of about 50 cents.

- Use your credit card, but only if you can repay the money when your monthly bill arrives. Online warriors might consider visiting their bank's website to immediately pay off a purchase charged to their credit cards.

- Shop around for a bank account package that takes it easy on people who like to use the most convenient ABM. Best example: Citizens Bank of Canada absorbs the network connection fee when its clients use outside ABMs (there are next to no Citizens Bank–branded machines), so you only pay the $1.50 surcharge. You can avoid even this fee by using bank machines in the Exchange network, which comprises many credit unions as well as banks such as Canadian Western Bank, HSBC Canada, and National Bank. A distinct advantage of the Exchange system is that, unlike Interac, you can make deposits, transfer money, and view your account balances at any ABM in the network, not just those of your home bank or credit union.

- Use cashback, a service offered by some retailers that allows you to add an extra amount to your bill when paying with a debit card, then receive that amount in cash.

- Avoid bank machines in casinos, bars, and tourist spots, because they tend to have the highest fees.

WARNING: SNEAK ATTACK

Operators of bank machines will always warn you if a fee applies on a withdrawal. Unfortunately, the warning always comes up once you've initiated the transaction and are likely to push ahead rather than abort. Here's the math explaining why you should try as much as possible to curb your use of ABMs operated either by banks with which you don't have an account or by no-name operators:

Typical "convenience fee" charged by the owner of the ABM (bank or no-name):	$ 1.50
Typical Interac network access fee charged by your own bank:	$ 1.50
Typical total cost	**$ 3.00**
Possible additional cost if your bank account package charges for withdrawals:	.50
Maximum cost:	**$ 3.50**

On a $60 cash withdrawal, these fees add up to a 5.8-percent service charge.

While most banks and credit unions maintain sizable branded networks of bank machines, you'll find a growing number of establishments with no-name, or "white label," ABMs. Is there a difference between brand-name and no-name ABMs? Nope. Both will soak you for the same surcharge of $1.50 or so. If you're curious why no-name machines are proliferating these days while bank-owned machines are less often seen in stores and other locations, it's because the white-label operators offer more favourable terms to retailers and land-lords than the tough-guy banks.

CHAPTER TWO IN ACTION

- Try online banking, if you haven't already, and attempt to make as much of your day-to-day transactions as possible this way.

  How you'll get better value for your dollar: People who use the Internet, phone, and bank machines for their transactions can easily pay less in fees and get better service through twenty-four-hour access to their accounts.

- Set up a high-interest savings account.

  How you'll get better value for your dollar: While paying zero in fees, the risk-free return on your savings will rise from around zero to a much more competitive level based on current interest rates.

- Contact your personal banker or do some research on the Internet to see whether you have the chequing account package that offers the best value for your personal style of banking.

  How you'll get better value for your dollar: With the right chequing account, you can cap your monthly costs and stop your bank from bleeding you with extra charges that can easily add up to more than $10 per month if you are not careful.

- Be careful about which bank machines you use.

  How you'll get better value for your dollar: The fees you pay when you use a bank machine not operated by your financial institution can easily add up to $3 or more per transaction. Do this three times a month and you have wasted $108 a year.

Conclusion: I know, I know. You're busy and you don't have the time to take a close look at whether you're getting as big a return as you could be on your savings and whether you're paying too much for your chequing account. Your bank was hoping you'd say that. Consumer inertia is the main reason why we continue to see so much money rotting away in savings accounts paying little or nothing, and so much being paid in fees for everyday banking.

THREE

CREDIT CARDS, LOANS, AND LINES OF CREDIT

Background briefing: There exists what I call the nanny school of personal finance writing, where readers must be admonished continually about the evils of credit. Me, I cut classes at this school. I embrace debt when necessary and, frankly, I think that it's an essential financial tool in a world where the average Canadian house costs more than $250,000 and economy cars can easily set you back $20,000. Paying with cash is great, but life's too short to deny yourself essentials and not-so-essentials while you save up.

Intelligent use of credit is the mark of a person who is truly financially savvy. Credit card debt is strictly verboten to these people because it's so hideously expensive, and loans are avoided as much as possible in favour of lines of credit, especially home-equity credit lines with their rock-bottom interest rates. Paying the least possible interest is the main objective when borrowing, with repayment flexibility a close second.

CREDIT CARDS

If you typically have a balance owing on your credit card instead of paying off your bill in full each month, then you've heard a million times how dumb it is to expose yourself to interest rates as high as 19.5 percent. It should be noted that low-rate cards with interest rates at about half this level are available, but you probably won't be interested because they almost never offer the rewards that are now a primary consideration in our choice of which cards to carry. But never mind. If you're going to incur debt you can't pay off immediately, do it with a line of credit and forget about credit cards of any type.

Think interest rates are all you should consider when it comes to controlling the cost of using credit cards? Not quite. Fees are often overlooked by card users, but they're as egregious in their own way as interest rates. Familiarize yourself with the various fees that can be charged, and resolve to avoid them.

The very existence of these fees may come as a surprise to people who sign up for credit cards on the basis of those seemingly fabulous reward programs that suggest lifestyles of the rich and clueless. Taken out a cash advance lately? Did you exceed your spending limit, make a purchase in a foreign currency, let your account become inactive, ask for a statement reprint or a copy of a sales slip? If so, you're likely paying sizable fees. Let's say you're on a trip outside the country and you use your credit card for a cash advance. The cost typically ranges from $3 to $5 for the credit cards offered by the big banks, while customers of other financial institutions could pay even more. One particularly expensive fee I've seen is 1 percent of the amount of the advance, with a minimum charge of $7.50 and no maximum.

Something else to watch out for is an administrative fee applied when you buy something priced in a foreign currency (this is applied on top of the currency exchange). Card issuers typically charge in the area of 2.5 percent. Exceeded your credit limit when making a purchase on your card? Many card issuers now levy a charge between $10 and $35 in such cases. Two other fees to be aware of: reprinting a statement or getting a copy of a sales slip will cost between $2 and $5.

POINTS TO PONDER

The biggest pitfall in credit card rewards is accumulating too few points to redeem for anything worthwhile, while paying $100 or more a year in fees. Increasingly, though, some of the more prominent loyalty programs are allowing their points to be swapped for those in other programs using a service called Points.com (www.points.com).

Using Points.com, you can keep track of how many points you've earned through loyalty programs such as Aeroplan, Esso Extra, and Hbc Rewards and then deploy those points to help earn the rewards you want most. For example, you can swap points from one program into another, or redeem points for magazine subscriptions and gift certificates for retail stores, hotels, and merchandise. Of course, there's a cost to all of this swapping, which is embedded in the exchange rate used between loyalty programs. Each program has its own economic value based on how much you have to spend to earn a point and what that point is worth. The Points.com website explains that each of its partner programs is allowed to decide what you can get with their points or miles. "As a result," the site warns, "all swaps may not meet your expectations."

Life's Rewards

You basically have two choices in credit cards these days: carry a no-fee, plain card with rewards that take eons to earn, or pay an annual fee for a gold or platinum card that offers the opportunity to earn flights and other travel, merchandise, or cash back. Which will you choose? People do love those gold cards, but they're a pure waste of money unless they're attached to a reward program you'll actually be able to use.

Whenever I write about credit card reward programs for my *Globe and Mail* personal finance column, I receive a barrage of questions from readers asking what the best rewards plan is. That's like asking me to name the best car or the best place to go on vacation. There's no definitive answer, because it depends on the views and needs of each individual. An ideal example of how this applies to credit card reward programs is Aeroplan, which is connected to several credit cards, including CIBC Aerogold Visa and American Express AeroplanPlus, and offers reward flights to locations served by Air Canada and its partner airlines.

I'm an Aeroplan member, and a pretty satisfied one at that. My wife and I, and sometimes our kids, have flown from our Ottawa home to Calgary, Orlando, New York, and Paris using at least one ticket redeemed through Aeroplan. Others haven't been so fortunate. They've tried repeatedly and unsuccessfully to book Aeroplan flights, only to be thwarted by the strict limits that Air Canada places on the number of Aeroplan seats per flight. What's our secret? We try to travel at non-peak times of the year and we are flexible on departure and return dates. Other people may not have that flexibility, or they may live in a part of the country where there's a smaller choice of flights and thus fewer opportunities to find an Aeroplan seat. For them, it's a waste of money to pay the $120 annual fee ($50 for additional cards) for CIBC Aerogold, or the $120 annual fee (no charge for supplemental cards) for Amex AeroplanPlus Gold.

Comparing Travel Rewards

So Aeroplan doesn't work for you. What are the alternatives? The last time I surveyed all of the travel cards out there—this type of reward program is among the most popular, which is why we'll focus on it here—I found four worthy alternatives:

- Bank of Montreal's Mosaik MasterCard with the Air Miles reward option (offers special benefits on WestJet Airlines)
- RBC Royal Bank Visa Platinum Avion
- ScotiaGold Preferred Visa
- TD Gold Travel Visa

I found RBC Avion to be a close second to Aeroplan in terms of delivering achievable reward flights and providing value for the annual membership fee. Check it out if you can't abide Aeroplan. BMO Mosaik Air Miles with WestJet benefits was a top choice for people who are happy with reward flights mainly within Canada. TD Gold Travel isn't the most productive in terms of turning your card spending into flights and other benefits, but it does offer an impressive and welcome level of flexibility in claiming travel rewards that go beyond mainly flights. Bank of Nova Scotia's offering is more of a generic gold card.

Before you settle on a card, be sure to check out secondary benefits such as travel or rental car insurance. It's also worth noting what other rewards are available in case you can't connect with the flight you want, not that the usual selection of merchandise is all that attractive in terms of getting good value for your reward dollars.

Skip These Credit Card Offers

Almost every offer a bank sends your way through mailings, ads on its websites, or other means is designed to do one thing: make money for the bank by providing an unnecessary service. Let's look at two examples.

1. Skip a payment: "You deserve a break!" my bank told me one day in a letter from its Visa card department, and offered an opportunity to skip that month's credit card payment. "Making a payment this month is optional and you don't need to call us to accept this offer!" My response, and the one I suggest you adopt when confronted with a similar offer for your credit card or mortgage? No way, no thanks.

Why banks even offer you the chance to skip a payment is hard to fathom, unless you're a cynic who believes it's to stealthily squeeze a little more revenue from you. When you skip a credit card payment, interest builds up on your entire month's charges at extremely high rates. My credit card happens to carry a rate of 19.5 percent, which is typical. As it happens, the balance on my card when I received the skip-a-payment letter was a hefty $6276.39 as a result of some home renovations. One month's share of the 19.5-percent annual interest on that amount would be about $102. Another reason to skip this offer? By skipping a payment, you may put yourself in a position where you fail to enjoy an interest-free period on the purchases you make in the following month. Credit cards typically start charging interest on your balance only after a period of time that spans the dates of your purchases and the due date of your monthly payment. But if you're carrying a balance from the previous month, some banks cancel the interest-free period and start charging interest as soon as you make a purchase.

Skipping a mortgage payment has even worse consequences. When you miss a mortgage payment, you extend the time it will take to pay off the loan because you haven't paid back the scheduled amount of principal. Worse, the interest you missed paying is added to what you owe, creating a situation in which you'll pay interest on interest. You'll resume your regular mortgage payments just as they were before, but the balance outstanding on your mortgage has been adjusted higher.

The worst thing about the skip-a-payment option is that banks pretend they're doing you a favour, when in fact they're helping themselves. It's a pattern of behaviour you see elsewhere, such as in those credit card convenience cheques that lure you into taking a cash advance on your card. Cash advances don't get an interest-free period like regular purchases on a card, so they're strictly for emergencies.

2. Credit card balance insurance: The only reason to take out credit card balance insurance is that you want to do your duty as a patriotic Canadian to bolster bank profits. There's simply no other justification for insuring the unpaid balance on your credit card against circumstances that prevent you from taking care of this debt—say, death or serious illness. To insure a continuing balance of $5000, you could end up paying monthly premiums totalling an astronomical $500 or so a year to your card issuer. You'd be far better off using that money to pay down your balance.

The federal government's Financial Consumer Agency of Canada says that at least twenty card issuers offer balance insurance, including all of the big banks, alternative banks such as President's Choice Financial and Citizens Bank of Canada, retailers such as Canadian Tire, Hudson's Bay Company, and Sears, and some gasoline retailers. The pitch is simple. If you become sick or disabled or lose your job, the minimum payment on your card statement will be made for you until you reach a maximum benefit of $5000 to $50,000, or you return to work (a twenty-four-month limit may apply). If you die or become critically ill, your card balance insurance will pay off the amount you owed when you got sick or died. The same dollar maximums apply.

Credit card balance insurance does have a theoretical benefit in that it may keep your credit rating in good standing by continuing your monthly payments without interruption. But in the real world, most people simply don't need balance insurance. If you have savings or liquid assets, you should be able to keep up with the minimum required payments on your bill for a time. Balance insurance is also superfluous if you already have a decent amount of life insurance coverage and/or disability or critical illness insurance. The main flaw of balance insurance is that it makes only the minimum payment for you if you become injured, disabled, or unemployed. This isn't too impressive when you consider that the required minimum payment may be as little as the interest owing that month plus $10.

Even if balance insurance is making your minimum payments, you'll still rack up interest on your outstanding balance
at rates of about 18 or 19 percent. Worse, some cards may automatically charge you interest on the next month's purchases if
you don't pay the previous month's bill in full.

SERIOUS BORROWING

Let's say you're about to do some renovation work on your
home and you'll need financing to pay the bill. Your options:

The Bonehead Move: Put It on Your Credit Card and Carry the Payments

This option assumes that you have a sufficiently high credit limit
and that any contractors involved are willing to let you charge
large amounts on a credit card. The minimum payments on your
card may be affordable, but anyone who pays 19.5-percent interest on major borrowings is a danger to himself or herself.

Advantages: Convenience and a big whack of reward points.

Disadvantages: Scary interest charges.

Your plan of attack: The only time you should use your credit
card for expenses of any type is when the money to pay the bill
is either in hand, or about to arrive. That way, you can generate
a lot of reward points and incur no interest.

The Old-Fashioned Move: Take Out a Loan

Loans are yesterday's borrowing tool because they give the bank
too much power. To start the loan process, you sit down with
your personal banking representative and explain how much
money you need and what you intend to spend it on. The bank

then considers this information as well as your credit history to decide on the interest rate it's prepared to offer you. The loan will be "open," so you can pay it off at any time, and you'll have some flexibility in determining the term of the loan. You can keep the term short and minimize your interest costs, though your monthly payments will be high, or you can stretch out the term and shrink your monthly payments.

Advantages: A loan puts you on a firm schedule to repay what you owe, with monthly payments that will be withdrawn directly from your bank account. Also, you may be able to get a loan when credit lines are unavailable to you because you lack sufficient income, have no credit history, or have a bad credit history. This would be done by having someone co-sign the loan for you, which means that the person will step up to repay the loan if you default.

Disadvantages: A loan is the most expensive way to borrow besides credit cards. You could easily pay 2 to 5 percentage points over the prime rate, which is the interest rate that banks charge their most creditworthy customers and the most frequently cited benchmark for borrowing costs. Also, loan rates are opaque, which is to say that there's no easy way to know what you'll pay other than to ask, negotiate, and then compare at other financial institutions.

Your plan of attack: Be totally upfront with the bank about your reasons for borrowing and ask for the best possible rate. Then, call a few other banks to see what they'll offer. *Do not* take out a loan without first shopping around, because rates vary widely. As I write this, the Canoe Money website (www.money.canoe.ca) shows a range of 6.95 percent to 9.25 percent for five-year car loans at major banks and credit unions. Loan rates are absolutely negotiable, by the way. One more hint: If you have a high-rate loan at your bank, you might be able to find cheaper rates elsewhere and shift the loan.

Something else to consider is the interest-rate environment. You could choose a fixed-rate loan to protect yourself against rate hikes, but you'll immediately pay a higher rate than with a floating-rate loan, which fluctuates with changes in the prime rate at your lender.

The Savvy Move: Unsecured Lines of Credit

A line of credit is best understood as a bank account topped up with a pre-set sum of money that you can dip into any time you like using a special cheque or making a withdrawal at a bank branch or through a bank machine. As soon as you do this, interest charges start to pile up at a rate determined when you established the credit line. You have total freedom to draw down your credit line, pay a bit back, and then draw down again, but you'll always face minimum monthly payments. These can be as low as interest only or as high as 2 or 3 percent of your outstanding balance, with a minimum of $50 or $60. The term *unsecured* refers to the fact that you haven't pledged any security for your borrowing.

Advantages: A line of credit is always at the ready and costs nothing until you use it. The rates are competitive—maybe 1 to 3 percentage points over prime—and it's easy to set up. In fact, it would be surprising if your bank hasn't invited you to establish a credit line already.

Disadvantages: The lack of structure in terms of repaying what you've borrowed may challenge less disciplined borrowers. One possible outcome is that you keep making just the minimum payment, which means you chip away at your principal a little or not at all while the interest meter keeps running. At worst, you could end up paying more interest than you would have with a loan.

Also, the convenience of credit lines can get you into trouble. The hassle of applying for a loan might stop you from an expensive impulse buy, whereas a line of credit actually facilitates this kind of consumption. One other disadvantage is vulnerability to rising interest rates—as the prime rate goes up, so do your borrowing costs.

Your plan of attack: Ask your banker what rate you qualify for and then try to squeeze it a bit lower. One or two points over prime seems fair for solid customers. Like credit cards, credit lines are best used to bridge a short-term gap between buying something and being able to afford it. Credit cards give you four weeks, but credit lines can give you much longer. If all you can really afford to pay are the interest charges, consider the structure of a loan, where principal and interest are blended into each payment and you're on a set track to retire the loan over a period of years.

The Savvier Move: Secured Lines of Credit

You'll probably recognize this type of borrowing if I call it by its more common name: the home-equity line of credit (bankers called it HELOC, pronounced HE-lock). The twist here is that you pledge some of the equity in your home as security for your borrowings, which in turn gives the lender the ability to offer a lower interest rate. Typically, that rate will be prime. Once your credit line is in place, you can borrow up to 75 percent of the appraised value or purchase price of your home, less any outstanding mortgage balance.

Here's a quick illustration of your borrowing power when you have a home-equity line of credit:

Value of your home:	$ 250,000
Your borrowing limit:	$ 187,500 (75% of $250,000)
Outstanding mortgage balance:	$ 125,000
You can borrow up to:	**$ 62,500**

(It's possible, though not advisable, to borrow more. Read on.)

Advantages: A secured line of credit is the cheapest way for the average person to borrow. If you use a credit line frequently and have the cash flow to pay your debts back quickly and easily, then a home-equity line of credit is a must.

Disadvantages: It can cost roughly $400 to $700 to set up a home-equity line of credit. You're essentially arranging a new mortgage—you'll only activate it when you draw down on your credit line—and that means legal fees and possibly an appraisal. Also, there's the theoretical risk you'll default and cause your lender to come looking for that piece of home equity you pledged. You'd have to screw up pretty badly for this to happen, however, because your lender would almost certainly show some flexibility at first in allowing you to pay what you owe.

An unlikely risk with home-equity credit lines, but one worth mentioning, is that the real estate market will head south just as you borrow heavily against your home equity. A massive decline in home prices could even wipe out all the equity you have in your home. Lenders aren't happy in such situations, but they likely won't take any action as long as you continue to make your monthly credit line payments and keep up with your mortgage.

Your plan of attack: Lenders may waive set-up fees on home-equity lines of credit if you commit to borrowing a set amount—$40,000, for example. The idea is to get you to start paying interest rather than sitting tight on a limit you never use. If you're not in a hurry, wait until your lender has a promotion so you can avoid those costly set-up fees, or find a bank that has a special deal. Only pay the full cost of the set-up fees as a last resort.

Something else to get straight with your lender is the interest rate on your credit line. If your credit rating isn't tip-top, you may have to pay a premium of a full percentage point or so over the prime rate. Remember, the whole point of a home-equity line of credit is the rock-bottom interest rate. If you can't get that rate, think twice.

One More Wrinkle, and a Costly One

Mortgages that cover more than 75 percent of the value of a home must be insured by the borrower to protect the lender in case of default. It's the same with home-equity credit lines. If you want to borrow up to 90 percent of your home's value, you'll need to get mortgage insurance on your credit line. This entails extra costs that will certainly lessen the low-rate appeal of a home-equity credit line. You'll have to pay an insurance premium of up to 2.5 percent of the amount of your credit line. The federal agency Canada Mortgage and Housing Corp., one of two providers of mortgage insurance, usually applies the amount of your premium to your credit line, so a $50,000 credit line becomes a $51,250 credit line, with a starting debt of $1250. You sure you really want to do this?

YOUR FINANCIAL PROFILE: LINES OF CREDIT

Online Warriors: People who comfortably use the Internet will have the easiest time using a credit line. Have some spare change rattling around in your chequing account? Online, it takes all of a few seconds to transfer that money into your credit line account to pay down your balance. Want to have some money ready and waiting in your chequing account to pay for something big? Just log on to your bank's website and transfer the money into chequing from your credit line.

Half and Halfers: You can manage your credit line by using phone banking, as well as online, and by using bank machines.

Traditionalists: Most credit lines now come with a chequebook, which provides a convenient way to pay big expenses.

The Not-So-Savvy but Comfortable Move: Refinance Your Mortgage

There's a way to borrow a big whack of money at a low rate and pay it back in such a way that you'll barely feel the pain. All you have to do is increase the amount of your mortgage, a move called refinancing. If your mortgage is coming up for renewal in a few months, your lender will probably welcome this idea. To start, decide how much you want to add to your balance owing. Then, ask your lender to renew your mortgage for the higher amount. If any legal or administrative fees apply, tell your lender to take a hike. After all, you're essentially volunteering to pay more interest than you were before—why should you pay added fees on top of this? If you want to grease the wheels to make your refinancing happen, tell your lender you're willing to sign up for a mortgage with a five-year term. Lenders love customers who make long-term commitments.

Advantages: Refinancings work well when you have a mortgage at a higher interest rate than you'll get when you renew. Although you're adding to your loan principal, the effect of lower rates could leave you in a position of paying only marginally more per month. The really comfortable thing about refinancing is that you have only your mortgage to worry about, without the complications of staying on top of a credit line as well.

Disadvantages: Mortgage refinancings can generate huge interest costs if you have many years left on your mortgage and don't plan to pay down the principal at all. If you have twenty years to go on your mortgage and top up the amount you owe by $50,000 so you can do some renovations, then you've essentially got yourself a twenty-year loan for $50,000.

Your plan of attack: To beat back the potentially astronomical interest charges from a refinancing, pay down your principal regularly, almost as if you had a line of credit. The quicker you whittle down the extra money you owe on your mortgage, the less interest you'll pay. Note: There's a bit of convenience in refinancing your mortgage that can make it worth incurring a little more interest than you'd pay with a credit line. With a credit line, you may be required to make minimum monthly payments, plus interest. Feeling a little squeezed one month and don't have the cash to make these payments? Tough. With a refinanced mortgage, on the other hand, you keep current on your repayments simply by making your regular monthly payments, but you have the flexibility to pay down your balance any time you like, subject to the terms of your mortgage.

By the way, the smart choice for refinanced mortgages is a variable-rate loan, which likely allows you to borrow at the prime rate minus a discount of 0.5 to 0.9 of a percentage point. If you're quick on the uptake, you'll realize that this is the cheapest borrowing you'll ever do. Remember how the super-savvy home-equity line of credit was pegged at prime? Well, here you're borrowing at less than prime. The major drawback, just to reiterate, is that you'll probably take longer to pay what you owe and thus run the risk of paying more interest than you would using other forms of borrowing.

Smart borrowers use mortgage refinancings for spending that will increase the value of their homes, not for new cars, trips, or trinkets. It is estimated that you can recoup approximately two-thirds of the cost of a remodelled bathroom when you sell your home. So, although you've increased the amount you owe on your home to put in a new john, you've theoretically raised the value of your residence as well.

A Quick Note about Debt Consolidation

If you're being nibbled to death by interest on credit cards, loans, and other borrowings with high interest rates, one option is to consolidate all of this debt and then throw it into your mortgage or home-equity line of credit. The interest rate on the combined debt will be a lot lower than on the individual borrowings, which means your monthly payments should decrease by a lot, improving your cash flow every month. Some points to be aware of if you do this: If you consolidate your debts into your mortgage, you could end up paying less interest in the near term but more over the long term. Also, if you're thinking of using a credit line, check to see what the minimum monthly payment would be on the amount you're intending to borrow. You don't want to stretch yourself too thin with payments you can't keep up with.

THE BORROWING LADDER

You're renovating your home. Here are your options for financing the job:

Your Choices	Typical Rate
Top rung—Home-equity line of credit	prime*
Second rung—Unsecured line of credit	prime + 2% or so
Third rung—Mortgage refinancing	normal mortgage rates apply**
Bottom rung—Credit cards	19%

* The prime rate is what lenders charge their best customers, and can be considered the best rate possible. The prime is directly influenced by the Bank of Canada's trendsetting overnight rate, which floats up and down according to the central bank's view on inflation and economic growth.

** Even if you get a very low mortgage rate, you could end up paying a lot of interest on your renovation loan because mortgages tend to be paid off over longer periods of time than credit lines.

YOUR CREDIT RATING, OR HOW TO KEEP THE CREDIT WELL
FROM RUNNING DRY

Your credit rating is your resumé as a borrower, and you can be certain that no one will lend you money without studying it from top to bottom. They'll look to see whether you've bounced cheques, failed to pay your monthly credit card bill on time, fallen behind on loans, had dealings with a collection agency, or declared bankruptcy. They'll also look to see how many credit cards you have, what loans you have outstanding, and whether you've co-signed a loan for someone else. All of this information is used by your lender to help decide, first, whether to offer you a mortgage, loan, or such and, second, what interest rate to offer you.

There are two ways to keep your credit file shipshape so that lenders will look at it and think, This is a person we want to do business with. The first, obviously, is to be disciplined in how you conduct your financial affairs. Don't let those credit card payments slide. Make sure you keep up with debt payments. Don't apply for a bunch of credit cards you'll never use because you earn better reward points with a card you already have. To guard against NSF cheques, get overdraft protection on your chequing account.

The second way to protect your credit rating is to order a copy of your credit file and peruse it for mistakes, which do crop up now and again. When you get your file, check it not only for accuracy, but also for clutter that suggests you're a serial borrower. If multiple credit cards that you never use are listed, call the card companies and cancel them.

CHECKING YOUR CREDIT FILE

Here's contact info for the keepers of credit data in Canada.

Equifax Canada

National Consumer Relations

P.O. Box 190, Station Jean-Talon,

Montreal, Quebec H1S 2Z2

Tel. (toll-free): 1–800–465–7166

Fax: (514) 355–8502

Website: www.equifax.ca

TransUnion Canada

All provinces except Quebec:

TransUnion

Consumer Relations Centre

P.O. Box 338 LCD 1

Hamilton, Ontario L8L 7W2

Tel. (toll-free): 1–866–525–0262

Fax: (905) 527–0401

Website: www.transunion.ca

For Quebec residents:

TransUnion (Echo Group)

1 Place Laval, Suite 370

Laval, Quebec H7N 1A1

Tel. (toll-free): 1–877–713–3393

Fax: (905) 527–0401

Website: www.transunion.ca

Northern Credit Bureaus Inc.

336 Rideau Boulevard

Rouyn-Noranda, Quebec J9X 1P2

Fax (toll-free): 1–800–646–5876

Website: www.creditbureau.ca

SOURCE: FINANCIAL CONSUMER AGENCY OF CANADA

CHAPTER THREE IN ACTION

- Get real with credit cards; never use them for carrying debts.

  How you'll get better value for your dollar: With interest rates as high as 19 percent or so, the cost of carrying debt on a credit card is quite possibly the biggest money waste in the entire field of personal finance. Use a credit card only to defer payment until your monthly statement arrives, and to generate reward points.

- Be choosy about which reward credit card you use.

  How you'll get better value for your dollar: Many reward cards charge annual fees of $120 or so, which is money wasted unless you are getting value in the form of useful rewards from your card.

- Arrange an unsecured or home-equity line of credit.

  How you'll get better value for your dollar: Credit lines are the cheapest and most flexible way for the average person to carry debt—better than a loan, and light years better than a credit card. By paying less in interest, you will be able to pay your debt off sooner and waste less of your cash flow on interest costs.

- Consider a loan in certain circumstances.

  How you'll get better value for your dollar: A loan will put you on a rigid schedule to pay what you owe, which works better for less disciplined borrowers than a credit line.

Conclusion: A few minutes spent studying the fine art of borrowing can save you thousands of dollars in interest over the years and ensure that your debts are paid off sooner. Want to keep things really simple? Use credit cards only if you can pay your debt when the monthly statement arrives, and set up a credit line (secured or unsecured) for the times when you need more time to pay off a debt.

FOUR

MORTGAGES

Background briefing: At some point in the past several years, the major banks lost control of the residential mortgage market. Banks still do the vast majority of lending in this area, but they don't have anywhere near the leverage they used to in setting rates and terms for clients. Whereas mortgage rate discounts were once a hush-hush, under-the-table thing, now they're so common that the big banks offer them upfront in some cases. In fact, the posted rates you see when you walk into a bank branch are as much a fiction as the car industry's manufacturer's suggested retail price. Unless you've got a weak credit rating or need only a tiny loan, don't even think about accepting a mortgage at the posted rate.

Three factors explain these changes in the mortgage market: the rising popularity of mortgage brokers, the easy availability of cheap rates from credit unions and alternative banks such as ING Direct and Citizens Bank of Canada, and a hot real estate market through much of this decade. Put them together and you get a lending environment in which creditworthy individuals should expect to get at least a full percentage point, and quite possibly a little more, off those posted bank rates, particularly on long-term mortgages of five years or more.

If you take just one piece of information from this chapter, let it be that you should *never* let a banker act as if he or she is doing you a favour by lending you money to buy a house. The true dynamic is that you're doing the bank a favour by taking out a mortgage. For one thing, mortgages are considered by banks to be an anchor product. If the bank has you as a mortgage customer, then credit lines, credit cards, and other lucrative forms of business may follow. For another thing, mortgages are very profitable. Banks have to make a profit, of course, but there's no need for you to pay more than your fair share through excessively high rates on your mortgage.

YOUR FINANCIAL PROFILE: MORTGAGES

Online Warriors: You'll have maximum flexibility in putting the information in this chapter to use because you'll be able not only to use the Internet to find the lowest rates and play with various borrowing calculators, but also to apply online for a mortgage if a virtual bank has the best rates.

Half and Halfers: Comparing rates online will give you all the information you need to ensure that you're getting the best possible deal from your lender.

Traditionalists: Even in this online age, most people end up talking to someone face to face or on the telephone when negotiating a mortgage. This chapter will provide you with guidelines to ensure that you get the right rate, even if you're not able to do some research on the Internet.

RENEWING A MORTGAGE

Arranging a new mortgage is one of life's milestones. I mean, how often do you sign your name and immediately assume responsibility for a chunk of debt measured in six figures? Once, maybe twice, in a lifetime for most people, which is why this chapter starts off with advice on renewing a mortgage, something you could easily do half a dozen times or more until your home is yours, free and clear. Here's some math from a former bank mortgage executive that emphasizes how important the mortgage renewal market is: as of mid-2006, the total amount of outstanding mortgages was worth roughly $660 billion, with about $80 billion of that representing new mortgages and the rest representing existing mortgages. Of that $580 billion or so in existing mortgages, about one-third ($193.3 billion) was up for renewal during the year. Given the rather immense amount of money being renewed each year, it's a surprise to hear from our former mortgage insider how many people sign and send back the mortgage renewal form sent to them by their banks, even though the rate being offered is not discounted at all. "If I told you how many people do this, you'd be floored," the insider said. "It's close to 30 percent."

Would you buy a car and pay the price listed on the sticker on the window? If you pay your bank's off-the-rack mortgage rate, you're making the same mistake, but maybe five times worse (car: $30,000; mortgage: $150,000). Never—repeat, *never*—simply renew a mortgage without trying to arrange a better deal. In fact, mortgage renewals should be treated as an opportunity, not as a formality. After living with whatever choices you made the last time you arranged a mortgage, you're now back in the cockpit with a chance to do better. Here's your game plan:

1. Research the market: Find out where mortgage rates are, and where they're expected to go. Then, see what deals lenders are offering.

YOUR FINANCIAL PROFILE:

RESEARCHING A MORTGAGE RENEWAL

Online Warriors and Half and Halfers: Cannex Financial Exchanges' website (www.cannex.com) is a definitive source of comparative data on interest rates, and some of it is free to the public. If you need a quick survey of rates at all major lenders, this is it. Next, try the websites of individual banks and credit unions to see if they have any promotions. The best place to get web addresses is the almighty Google search engine—the Canadian version can be found at www.google.ca. You can find mortgage brokers by looking them up in the Yellow Pages—many brokers now include web addresses in their ads.

Traditionalists: A phone call to a few lenders or, better, mortgage brokers should give you a quick-and-dirty market survey.

2. Call, email, or visit your lender: Who knows, you may be offered a great deal right off the top, thus ending the renewal process. Failing that, get your lender's best offer and go elsewhere to see what you can do to beat it. And, yes, you can conduct mortgage negotiations by email. I once renewed my mortgage through an exchange of emails over several days with a mortgage rep at one of the banks I patronize. We never met face to face.

3. Choose your lender: It's always easiest to keep your mortgage where it is, so give your bank one last chance to hang on to your business. Frankly, the convenience of staying put is probably worth an incrementally higher interest rate.

If your current lender won't deliver the rate you want, then you'll find other banks, credit unions, and mortgage brokers eager to win your business. Often, they'll demonstrate their eagerness by absorbing any legal and administrative costs involved in transferring your mortgage (these could add up to several hundred dollars otherwise). As well, your existing lender may charge a mortgage discharge fee of $150 to $250. Be sure to ask your new lender to pick up the tab—remember, it's competitive out there.

THE IDEAL MORTGAGE

If you want a quick and easy-to-follow guide to the ideal mortgage, try a book called *The Perfect Mortgage* by real estate lawyer Alan Silverstein. I've been consulting Alan for more than ten years for stories and columns on mortgages, and he's great at explaining mortgage technicalities in a simple way. For me, though, an ideal mortgage is simply one that comes with the lowest possible interest rate for the term you want, be it variable rate, six-month, five-year, or ten-year. Sure, there are other factors, such as your ability to pay down the principal and portability (transferring the mortgage when you move to a new home). But if you had to isolate one single measure that makes a mortgage more bearable, it would have to be a low rate.

Low Rates Are within Your Grasp

There was a time not too long ago when only a display of negotiating virtuosity got you a discount of a full percentage point on your fixed-rate mortgage. Today, these deals are so commonplace that you'll find banks promoting them in flyers enclosed with your daily newspaper. Forget negotiating or having a "relationship" with the bank in question—these specials are open to anyone with a pulse and a decent credit rating.

- **Example no. 1:** Toronto-Dominion Bank's TD Canada Trust branches offered a special 4.99 percent on five-year mortgages in one recent spring, which compared to a posted rate of 6.05 percent. " . . . Save with our special mortgage offers," a TD flyer said.

- **Example no. 2:** Canadian Imperial Bank of Commerce has in the past had a "Better Than Posted" mortgage product that offered a large discount of up to 2.01 percentage points for the first nine months and then a smaller discount of up to 1 point for the remainder of the term. "This is a fixed-rate mortgage that gives you guaranteed rate reductions on our posted rates—without having to negotiate!" CIBC's website said.

- **Example no. 3:** Royal Bank of Canada's website not too long ago had a section headlined "Our Best Offers," where you could find details on a five-year 4.99-percent mortgage available for a limited time. The posted rate at that time was 6.05 percent.

While there's no question that banks have become a lot easier to deal with if you need a mortgage, you still require some savvy to get the best possible deal. Here are some key points:

- Don't be awed into submission by special deals, because they're not the last word on pricing. If you have a good relationship with your bank, don't hesitate to ask for a little extra discounting. You'll have more leverage if you're seeking a long-term mortgage of five years or more, and if the closing date for your home purchase is near at hand. With today's interest rate volatility, banks may be less willing to commit to a super-low rate on a mortgage they won't actually fund for a couple of months.

- Don't put any stock in posted mortgage rates, even though all banks have them. Posted rates sometimes differ from bank to bank, but they're just trivia. Discounted real market rates are where it's at.

- Teaser rates—super-low rates that apply only for the first few months of your mortgage and then convert to a higher rate— generally qualify as flim-flammery. If you analyze these deals, you'll generally find that it's better to negotiate your own discount.

- It's illegal for banks to require that you bring them a certain piece of business if you want to get a mortgage—this is called tied selling—but they may be more willing to offer the rate and terms you want if you give them, say, an RRSP account. If you're willing to do something like this to cinch a mortgage deal, go ahead. But don't make any changes that will hurt you financially or cause undue hassle. Remember, there are many banks, credit unions, trust companies, and mortgage brokers you can approach if your bank won't give you the deal you want.

MEET SOME ALTERNATIVE MORTGAGE LENDERS

You already know the Big Six banks. How could you not, when their branches are as ubiquitous as lampposts across the Canadian landscape? Alternative lenders have a much lower profile, often because they're credit unions trying to run as frugally as possible, or online banks that conduct business by telephone, fax, email, and through their websites. Here are some alternative lenders you should know about:

- **Cervus Financial:** A publicly traded lender that specializes in high-ratio mortgages (ones with less than a 25-percent down payment) and works through mortgage brokers. www.cervus.com; 877–462–3788
- **Citizens Bank of Canada:** An online bank that figured prominently in Chapter Two because of its attractive banking services, it is also a mortgage lender with rates that solidly undercut the big banks on a consistent basis. www.citizensbank.ca; 888–708–7800
- **FirstLine Mortgages:** "Why pay retail?" this lender asks on its website. FirstLine is owned by Canadian Imperial Bank of Commerce. www.firstline.com; 800–970–0700
- **First National Financial:** A small independent player that only offers mortgages. www.fnfc.com; 866–488–0794
- **ICICI Bank Canada:** The Canadian arm of a major bank from India. www.icicibank.ca; 888–424–2422
- **ING Direct:** The online bank that popularized the high-interest savings account in Canada also offers mortgages, as well as lines of credit. www.ingdirect.ca; 800–464–3473
- **President's Choice Financial:** An online banking venture offered by the supermarket chain Loblaw Cos. and CIBC. www.pcfinancial.ca; 888–872–4724
- **Your neighbourhood credit union:** Some credit unions offer pretty much the same rates as the banks, but others are admirably aggressive in the way they price mortgages. Stop in and see what they have to offer.

MORTGAGE RATES: A SNAPSHOT IN TIME

Here's a comparison of posted five-year mortgage rates that I found as I was writing this book. It's designed to show you how rates differ between the big banks and other lenders. Check with each lender for up-to-date rates. Also, note that posted big-bank rates are almost always negotiable.

Bank of Montreal	6.75%
Bank of Nova Scotia	6.75
Canadian Imperial Bank of Commerce	6.75
Cervus Financial	5.40
Citizens Bank of Canada	5.35
FirstLine Mortgages	5.65
ICICI Bank Canada	5.30
ING Direct	5.30
President's Choice Financial	5.37
Steinbach Credit Union (Manitoba)	5.30
Royal Bank of Canada	6.75
Toronto-Dominion Bank	6.75

SOURCE: CANNEX FINANCIAL EXCHANGE, WWW.CANNEX.COM

PREPARING FOR BATTLE

When talking about mortgages with a lender, never ask a question to which you don't already know the answer. The reason is that lenders have a tendency to provide information that benefits them as much as you. They're sometimes willing to lend you more for a mortgage than you should borrow if you want to keep some flexibility in your family finances, and they'll have their own ideas about the best term and rate for you. For an intelligent exchange of ideas to occur, you need to have answers beforehand.

Back-of-the-envelope calculations are pretty much out of the question here, because mortgages are so mathematically complex, but help is readily accessible on a number of websites. Most are operated or sponsored by mortgage brokers or financial institutions, but the information is impartial because you're in charge of the data used for the calculations. Let's start with affordability, a source of anxiety to many a new home-buyer. Visit the Mortgage Centre at www.mortgagecentre.com, then click on Mortgage Tools and select Mortgage Calculators, where you'll find a Mortgage Qualifier that can illustrate your ability to afford a home you've got your eye on.

Key variables here are the price of the house and your gross debt service ratio, which is the percentage of your total income required to cover the principal and interest on your mortgage payment and property taxes. Most lenders will allow 32 percent, but you may find this level too high when you consider the additional costs of hydro, heating, and other utilities. If you want to be more conservative, try using a debt service ratio of, say, 25 percent to see how much home you can afford.

For a different approach to affordability, try the online mortgage calculator offered by Canada Mortgage and Housing Corp., in the Consumers area of its website at www.cmhc-schl.gc.ca (click on Buying a Home). Supply your financial particulars, including the amount of your down payment, and you'll be told the maximum house price you can afford. Note that this calculator uses a different debt service ratio, this one stipulating that your total debt costs, including housing and other debts, should not consume more than 40 percent of your gross monthly income.

Next up, there's the question of what term and rate to go with. The CanadaMortgage.com site at www.canadamortgage.com has a calculator in its tools area that allows you to compare two rates head to head. Say your bank was offering you 5.5 percent on a $100,000 five-year mortgage, and another lender was offering 5.15 percent. The calculator says that the lower rate would save you slightly more than $1400 over the five years through lower monthly payments and a lower balance at the end of the term.

There are a few other variables to consider in creating an ideal mortgage, including the down payment (the larger, the better) and the amortization period (the shorter, the better). The financial planning firm Fiscal Agents (www.fiscalagents.com) offers some useful tools in these areas.

One thing to be aware of with all of these calculators is that they won't give you numbers that correspond to what your lender will offer. There are nuances to financial institutions' calculations that an online tool cannot account for. Still, these online resources will give you basic information that will help you in making mortgage decisions. Don't talk to your lender without it.

YOU AND YOUR LENDER: GETTING COZY

Now that you've crunched some numbers (or been crunched by the numbers, given today's housing costs), it's time to visit your lender to arrange your mortgage. Be upfront about everything, including the price range you're looking at, and be sure to ask your lender for her or his take on the market and what other clients are doing. At best, you'll get some useful insight on the rate environment or real estate market; at worst, you'll be able to gauge the BS factor you'll face in negotiations over rates and terms.

Arriving at a mutually acceptable rate is only part of the negotiation. As well, you must secure a commitment from your lender to hold your rate for as long as possible. The usual range is anywhere from 60 to 120 days.

MORTGAGE BROKERS, OR KEEPING THE BIG BANKS HONEST

I often wonder why mortgage brokers aren't more popular. It could be that people are needlessly worried that brokers charge fees for the services they provide in linking clients to a wide variety of potential lenders, or maybe people are put off by a lack of familiarity with who brokers are, how they work, and where the mortgage money they supply comes from. There may even be a bit of wariness about mortgage brokers in general. Brokers have made the news a few times over the years for things like breach of trust and financial mismanagement, but the victims were mostly people who invested in mortgages and not those who borrowed money.

YOUR FINANCIAL PROFILE: MORTGAGE BROKERS

Online Warriors and Half and Halfers: A Google.ca search for mortgage brokers should turn up many broker websites, where you'll almost always find an "our best rates" page. You may be able to do some of the mortgage application process online.

Traditionalists: Pick up the Yellow Pages, look under "mortgage brokers," and call a few different firms to compare rates and find someone who sounds knowledgeable and pleasant to work with.

The mortgage brokerage business has actually grown hugely in recent years, but its share of the market was still around 30 percent at mid-decade, compared with roughly 70 percent in the United States. Obviously, many Canadians still go to their usual bank for a mortgage and take whatever deal is offered, give or take a few concessions made during negotiations. There are three good reasons to consider visiting a mortgage broker as well as your own bank when you need a mortgage:

1. To secure the lowest rate possible, mortgage brokers can place your mortgage with a variety of lenders, some of them brand-name financial institutions and others small players that don't deal directly with the public (interestingly, some of these low-profile lenders are owned by the big banks).
2. Mortgage brokers almost always charge nothing for this service.
3. Unlike banks, mortgage brokers never make their best rates contingent on your bringing them different lines of business such as your registered retirement savings plan.

TACTICAL TIP

Even if you're not sold on the idea of using a mortgage broker, it might be worthwhile to visit one to get a rate commitment that you can wave in front of an account representative at your usual bank, should the need arise. Nothing counters your bank's reservations about offering a great rate like a firm offer for that same rate from someone else.

There were about 10,000 mortgage brokers and agents (employees of brokerage firms) working in Canada at mid-decade, up from several hundred or so in the early 1990s. Brokers must be licensed provincially, but agents may or may not require a licence of their own. Finding a mortgage broker is easy—check the Yellow Pages, or ask for a referral from the real estate agent who is working with you to buy a home. How do you know if you've got a reputable broker? Start by asking about his or her experience and accreditation. The Canadian Institute of Mortgage Brokers and Lenders (CIMBL), the professional group for mortgage brokers, offers a designation called AMP, for accredited mortgage professional, which can only be held by people who have successfully completed a recognized proficiency course or passed a CIMBL exam, and who have passed a CIMBL ethics course. There are more than 3200 AMP-accredited brokers, and you can find them listed on the CIMBL website at www.cimbl.ca.

Asking about AMP accreditation is especially important these days, what with more and more people working as mortgage brokers. A report on the mortgage brokerage business by a financial-industry consulting firm showed that even brokers themselves were concerned about all the newcomers in their line of business. "Despite facing an uncertain interest-rate environment and housing market, the threat posed by the flood of inexperienced mortgage brokers is viewed as one of the biggest challenges facing the mortgage brokerage industry," the report said. In other words, brokers are worried about rookies and slackers ruining the reputation of their profession. Sounds like a legitimate concern, so don't deal with just anyone calling himself or herself a mortgage broker.

Other than when they work with credit-challenged clients, mortgage brokers provide a free service. They make their money in commissions paid by the lender, which could range from 0.6 to 1.5 percent of the amount borrowed. One lender, Cervus Financial, pays an ongoing fee to the broker, just like mutual fund companies do to investment advisers. These payments are made directly by the lender to the broker, with no involvement by the borrower. Invisible compensation for mortgage brokers works well in that the customer pays nothing but also gets a low interest rate. Still, it's legitimate to ask what commission your broker is making from a particular mortgage lender, and how that compares with the compensation offered by other financial institutions.

SAVING THE VARIABLE-RATE WAY

Borrowers may never see a more perfect opportunity to capitalize on the savings potential of variable-rate mortgages than they did during the declining interest rate environment of

2000 through early 2005. Variable-rate mortgages use the major banks' prime lending rate as a reference, usually with a discount of at least half a percentage point (in banking jargon, this is "prime minus a half"). The prime is a floating rate, which means that it moves up and down over time, depending on the broader trend for interest rates. Practically speaking, this means that if banks cut their prime rate by 0.25 of a percentage point, people with variable-rate mortgages see their rate fall by a quarter of a point. If the prime falls a cumulative 3.75 percentage points, as it did between 2000 and 2004, then variable-rate mortgage holders benefit every step of the way. Yes, the opposite is true, too. If rates are rising, so are your borrowing costs.

The ability to ride interest rates lower is one reason why variable-rate mortgages accounted for up to 40 percent of mortgage renewals at mid-decade. Another is that wherever the prime rate happens to be at any given point in time, it's very often lower than rates for fixed-rate mortgages with a five-year term (while three- and four-year terms are available, most people choose five years if they don't opt for a short-term or variable-rate mortgage). Canadian Imperial Bank of Commerce has estimated that the long-term average spread, or gap, between the prime rate over five-year loans is 1.5 percentage points.

DETAILS, DETAILS

Here are a few points about how variable-rate mortgages work:

- Your lender will ensure that you can afford mortgage payments at the three-year rate (typically, this will be higher than that on a variable-rate mortgage), just to see whether you can handle a rise in interest rates.
- Rates are adjusted each month, as necessary, to reflect changes in the prime.
- Your payments may change when rates do.
- Payments can also be fixed, so that a rise in rates means that a *little* more of your payment goes to interest than principal, and a decline in rates means that a *little* more money goes to principal than interest.
- You generally have lock-in privileges, which means you can convert your variable-rate mortgage to a fixed-term mortgage without a penalty.
- Prepayment privileges are pretty much the same as with fixed-rate mortgages—you may be able to repay 15 or 20 percent of your outstanding balance once each year, or increase your payments by those amounts.

A couple of studies have been done on the efficacy of variable-rate mortgages, and we'll explore them in a moment. But let me say right off the top that I think these mortgages are the best choice for experienced borrowers who want to reduce the staggeringly large interest charges associated with a mortgage by as much as possible.

The Case for Variable-Rate Mortgages

A study conducted several years ago by Moshe Milevsky, a finance professor at York University's Schulich School of Business, estimated that choosing a fixed five-year mortgage over a variable-rate mortgage would have cost an extra $22,000 in interest on average between 1950 and 2000, assuming a fifteen-year amortization period. The study—partly funded by Manulife Financial, a mortgage lender with a variable-rate product called Manulife One—found that consumers often would have been better off borrowing at prime than taking a five-year term between 1950 and 2000 (remember, variable-rate mortgages are pegged to the prime). How often? A little more than 88.6 percent of the time. Why? Because the prime rate is typically a good deal lower than five-year mortgage rates.

More recently, Canadian Imperial Bank of Commerce economist Benjamin Tal reported that since the 1970s, variable-rate mortgages outperformed five-year mortgages 88 percent of the time. Assessing a rising-rate interest environment in the first half of 2006 that had squeezed the differential between prime and the five-year rate to about half the normal level, he still was able to forecast that variable-rate mortgage holders would save hundreds of dollars in interest by the end of 2007.

The Case against Variable-Rate Mortgages

With a fixed-rate mortgage, you're buying a kind of insurance against rising borrowing costs over the term of the loan, be it one year, five years, ten years, or whatever. Variable-rate mortgages provide no such protection. The prime rate, the reference rate for variable-rate mortgages, will change whenever the

Bank of Canada adjusts its trendsetting overnight rate. There are eight opportunities throughout the year for the overnight rate to be changed, which means a lot of potential volatility for the prime and, in turn, your mortgage. If you can't live comfortably with the idea that the interest rate on your mortgage could creep steadily higher over a period of time, then a variable-rate loan isn't worth the aggravation. Call this the emotional argument against variable-rate mortgages.

Now for the statistical argument. In a 2003 study, an economist with the federal agency Canada Mortgage and Housing Corp. found that the interest costs of a five-year mortgage were pretty much the same as those attached to a riskier variable-rate mortgage, providing you got a hefty rate discount. The study found that between 1993 and mid-1996, the five-year mortgage was costlier in terms of interest costs. Over the next seven years, however, five-year rates were close to those on variable-rate mortgages, and often they were even lower.

What to make of all this: The single biggest issue in determining whether you will save with a variable-rate mortgage is where interest rates are headed at the time you're taking out your loan. If rates are in a downtrend, as they were through the first half of this decade, then you're going to save, big time. If rates are flat, you'll still likely save considerably. And if rates are rising? I still think you'll save, though maybe not dramatically. Yes, there are times when the prime rate may rise above the five-year rate. But these periods don't tend to last long. When they're over, the prime will settle below the five-year rate and you'll once again be saving money. Something else to consider is that the likelihood of an interest-rate surge along the lines of what we saw in the early 1980s and early 1990s seems extremely remote. Central banks have shown in recent years that they are much more skilled than they used to be at raising interest rates to forestall inflation. Net result: You don't have to worry about 21-percent mortgage rates like we saw in 1982.

The Fine Points of Variable-Rate Mortgages

Monthly payments: Your biggest concern in taking out a variable-rate mortgage is that rates will shoot up and your monthly payments will become unmanageable. Smart borrowers, and lenders, protect themselves in a couple of ways.

First, your lender should ensure that you can afford mortgage payments pegged to a three-year rate, which should be a fair bit higher than the payments for a variable-rate mortgage. The point here is to provide an affordability buffer—if rates rise, you know you will be able to afford it. That's the theory, anyway. In reality, you'll probably become comfortable making payments on your variable-rate mortgage at a certain level and then find you're pinched if you have to pay more. One way around this problem is to ask your lender to increase the payments on your variable-rate mortgage above what they should be, based on current rates.

Let's say you have a variable-rate mortgage at 4.5 percent and the five-year mortgage rate is 6 percent. By putting yourself on the payment schedule required for a 6-percent mortgage, you'd protect yourself against a 1.5-percentage-point increase in the prime rate. In other words, prime would have to rise 1.5 points before your bank would contact you to say that it's time to raise your payments. The added bonus of doing this is that the extra amount on your payments will go directly against your mortgage principal and thus reduce the total interest bill over the life of your mortgage.

Wheeling and dealing: As variable-rate mortgages gained popularity, lenders had to become more competitive to differentiate their products in this category. Net result: It's standard for variable-rate mortgages to be sold with sizable rate discounts off prime.

VARIABLE-RATE MORTGAGES: WHAT THE BANKS OFFER, AND WHAT YOU SHOULD HOLD OUT FOR

The offer: Here's an excerpt from some promotional information that once appeared on TD Canada Trust's website to publicize one of its variable-rate mortgage products: "Take out a five-year, closed variable interest rate mortgage and you can pay the TD Mortgage Prime rate for the full five-year term of your mortgage. That can add up to thousands of dollars in savings."

Your counter-offer: Sounds lovely, but I'll take prime minus 0.9 of a percentage point, please.

You might settle for: Prime minus 0.75 or 0.5 of a percentage point, at the very least.

Discounting on variable-rate mortgages is very similar to discounting on all other mortgages—the very best deals are generally available from mortgage brokers, but banks and credit unions offer competitive rates as well, providing you do your research and have the right frame of reference to evaluate what is being offered. As I write this, the variable-rate discounts available range from prime minus 0.9 of a percentage point at a few different mortgage brokers to prime minus 0.5 or 0.25 of a point at some big banks.

You'll also find that some lenders offer super-low teaser rates on variable-rate mortgages, and these numbers can sometimes be so tiny they'll make your head spin right around. These offers always look the same: a strikingly low rate is offered in big type, with an asterisk beside it. Example: One particular mortgage broker has offered prime minus 2.51 points on a five-year variable-rate mortgage, which becomes prime minus 0.4 after the first three months. A general rule with teaser rates is that you're better off with a big discount that lasts the entire term of the mortgage. If there's an asterisk beside the rate, the offer you're looking at is quite likely a come-on.

Lock-in privileges: If you're especially interested in this aspect of variable-rate mortgages, perhaps this product really isn't for you. Yes, it's possible that interest rates could soar, and that locking in your variable-rate mortgage could protect you from the worst of this. Frankly, though, you're almost certainly going to be better off if you endure the pain of an interest rate surge for a while and then ride the inevitable decline that follows (if rates soar, they will choke the economy and thus send borrowing costs lower).

The key thing to discuss with your lender regarding lock-in privileges is the term and rate available when you lock in. You may well face restrictions on the term. For example, you might have to accept a mortgage term of three years or longer. Or, you might have to take a term that is equal to or longer than the period remaining on your variable-rate mortgage. If you think that locking in is something you might well do, then make it a point to ask your lender what type of rate you would get in such a situation. Only a minority of lenders automatically spell out the rate discount you'll get when you lock in (for example, posted rate minus 1.15 percentage points for a five-year term). Ask your lender for a commitment in writing that you'll get the posted rate minus an agreed-upon discount.

Term: Variable-rate mortgages are often sold with five-year terms these days, especially in cases where a promotion offers a discount off the prime rate. Shorter-term variable-rate mortgages are available if you shop around.

Open vs. closed: Typically, a variable-rate mortgage will be closed, which means you'll face a stiff penalty if you want to pay it off in full and walk away before your term is over. Some institutions offer open variable-rate mortgages, where you can bail out at any time with complete freedom. Note that open variable-rate mortgages won't be available with the same level of discounting as closed versions (this applies to open mortgages of any type, by the way).

A Different Spin on the Variable-Rate Mortgage: The BA Mortgage

We're getting into some pretty arcane territory here, so brace yourself. While the typical variable-rate mortgage is priced off the prime, another version of this product is pegged to a more obscure standard called the banker's acceptance (BA) rate. This, in simplified terms, is the rate that financial institutions charge each other for short-term borrowings. What's the appeal of using the banker's acceptance rate? For starters, it's much lower than prime.

As I write this, the thirty-day BA rate is 3.55 percent and the ninety-day rate is 3.67 percent. The prime, by comparison, is 5.25 percent. Should you sign up for a BA mortgage right away? Not so fast. Just as variable-rate mortgages tied to the prime are commonly discounted by 0.5 to 0.9 of a percentage point, so are BA mortgages marked up by 0.85 to 1 point. Do the math: prime minus 0.85 is 4.4 percent; the thirty-day BA plus 0.85 percent is, wait for it, 4.4 percent.

So what, exactly, is the appeal of a BA mortgage? At certain times, usually when rates are moving lower or are stable, the marked-up rate on a BA mortgage can be a few hundredths of a percentage point lower than the discounted rate on a variable-rate mortgage pegged to the prime. Over the course of a twenty-five-year mortgage, the savings we're talking about here typically add up to several hundred dollars. You'll have to decide whether that's enough to warrant a move into a mortgage priced off an interest rate most people have never heard of that is tracked only by people who work on Bay Street.

If you're serious about a BA mortgage, be sure to ask whether the thirty-day or ninety-day rate is being used. Some lenders use one, some the other. Then, ask about the markup and have a comparison drawn to a discounted, prime-based mortgage to see where the value is at the moment. By the way, BA mortgages are typical variable-rate mortgages in that you can lock in to a fixed-rate mortgage at any time without penalty.

Son of Variable-Rate Mortgage: The Flexible Mortgage Account

The flexible mortgage account—Manulife One is by far the most popular version in Canada—is a concept that Britons and Australians have adopted enthusiastically and Canadians have warily begun to try in increasing numbers. Think of these products as a combination of a variable-rate mortgage, line of credit, and chequing account. In very simple terms, your mortgage and any other borrowings you have sit as a gigantic overdraft in your account. Any time you add cash—say, when your paycheque is deposited—it works to reduce your balance owing.

To see the benefit here, you have to understand that interest on your mortgage is calculated daily, which means that cash deposited in the account for even a few days will temporarily reduce your balance owing, and thus your interest bill. Over the years, this continual applying of your cash assets against your mortgage balance should help you pay off your mortgage years earlier and with much less interest. Manulife One claims you can pay off your mortgage six or seven years sooner by doing this, while the Virgin One account offered in Britain claims: "We've proved that it would save eight out of every 10 people thousands of pounds over their lifetime."

One negative with flexible mortgage accounts is that you generally have to peg your mortgage rate at prime, without any discount. Right away, you're at a disadvantage relative to a traditional variable-rate mortgage, which almost certainly would be discounted by 0.5 to 0.9 of a percentage point. Another disadvantage is that it's almost too easy to borrow money. The typical flexible mortgage account gives you access to 75 percent of the value of your home, but there are versions that will let you have 90 percent. This money is completely accessible at all times through your regular bank account, which may prove too much of a temptation for some people to resist. The net result of serial borrowing using a flexible mortgage account is that you never reduce your mortgage balance and thus pay much more interest than you need to.

YOUR FINANCIAL PROFILE: FLEXIBLE MORTGAGE ACCOUNTS

Online Warriors and Half and Halfers: You should have no trouble at all managing this kind of account, provided you buy into the concept. *Traditionalists:* Given that by far the largest player in this product category is Manulife Bank, which has no branch network, you may find that a flexible mortgage account is too inflexible for your needs. One thing to note is that Royal Bank branches will accept deposits for Manulife One accounts.

For careful borrowers, the benefits of a flexible mortgage account outweigh the detriments. First, all of your cash on hand will count against your mortgage balance. If you've got significant savings kicking around in a few different accounts and maybe some Canada Savings Bonds, you're better off throwing it all into a flexible mortgage account and having it count against your mortgage until you need to make a withdrawal. Even having a couple of paycheques regularly deposited into your account will help eat away at your mortgage. The more subtle advantage of a flexible mortgage account is simplicity. Credit lines, savings accounts, chequing accounts, and a mortgage all become one, which means you do not have to worry about shunting money back and forth to ensure that you're keeping up with all of your debts and savings requirements.

In addition to Manulife One, two other financial players offer flexible mortgage accounts as this book is being written. One is National Bank of Canada, which calls its product the All-In-One account, and the other is B.C.-based credit union Envision Financial, which has given its flexible mortgage account the catchy name of Redfrog. Don't expect the major banks to offer flexible mortgage accounts any time soon. They make a lot more money if customers do their borrowing the conventional way—through credit cards, loans, credit lines, and such.

THREE QUESTIONS TO ASK IF YOU'RE INTERESTED IN A FLEXIBLE MORTGAGE ACCOUNT

1. What are the set-up fees? Costs for legal work and such can run to several hundred dollars, but financial institutions will sometimes waive all or most of these fees. Frankly, I wouldn't set up one of these accounts if I had to pay hundreds of dollars in set-up fees.

2. What are the monthly account fees? Manulife has charged $14 per month, while National Bank and Envision have no fees. Also, ask whether fees apply if you exceed a set number of transactions per month.

3. What documentation is provided to show how quickly you're paying down your mortgage? Manulife, for example, provides a monthly statement that shows how much money went in and out of your account, and provides a graph to show your declining mortgage balance.

A SLAM-DUNK WAY TO SAVE MONEY ON YOUR MORTGAGE
AND OTHER BORROWINGS

It's simple—take a pass when your friendly personal banker offers you the opportunity to insure your mortgage, loan, or line of credit against death or critical illness. Banks sell this type of insurance because it's a nifty little money maker, and they're politely aggressive when pitching it to clients. You may find that you actually have to initial a document to decline mortgage insurance, rather than simply decline it verbally. It's almost as if buying this kind of insurance is the natural way of things, so you need to sign off on the alternative because it's such a foolish thing to do.

Watch out, because you'll probably be tempted to say yes to the offer of insurance. After all, a loan, mortgage, or fully drawn-down credit line could be quite a burden to leave your family with if you died. Truth be told, you should have some insurance to cover eventualities like this. So, after you say no to the bank, call some insurance salespeople or brokers and ask for quotes on plain old term life insurance.

If you're a healthy non-smoker with no medical issues, you may well end up paying less for term life insurance. In some cases, bank insurance may cost less, or be easier to get, if you have medical issues or you smoke. Either way, term life is the better option because of the flexibility it offers. When you sign up for bank-offered mortgage insurance, the beneficiary is the bank. If you die, the bank gets paid and your survivors keep the house without a mortgage. With a term life policy, you can designate anyone as the beneficiary. Just as importantly, that beneficiary can do whatever he or she wants with the money paid out by the policy. Your term coverage also stays with you regardless of what you do with your mortgage. If you renegoti-ate your mortgage or blow off one bank for another one, your mortgage insurance ends and you'll have to arrange new cover-age, possibly at a higher price.

There's a value-for-money issue as well when comparing bank-sold insurance and term life. If you keep rolling over your mortgage with the same bank for twenty-five years, the premi-ums on the insurance sold by the lender remain steady for the life of the mortgage. At the same time, though, the amount you owe the bank is shrinking as you make your payments. In other words, you're paying a level amount for a shrinking level of cov-erage. Banks say the declining loan balance is factored into the setting of your premiums, but you'll still end up paying for neg-ligible coverage in the final days of your mortgage.

Another time to say no thanks to your bank is when it offers you mortgage critical illness insurance, which provides a lump sum of money if you are diagnosed with diseases or medical conditions ranging from cancer and heart disease to multiple sclerosis and Parkinson's disease. This is a somewhat tougher call because the critical illness coverage sold by banks may be cheaper than coverage you would get from big insurance com-panies. The problem is, you also get less coverage from the banks. Typically, cancer, heart disease, and stroke are the only conditions covered. These diseases account for about 85 per-cent of critical illness insurance claims, but it's worth noting that critical illness policies offered by insurance companies may include more than twenty conditions.

Here are some final thoughts on ways to ensure that you pay the least for the best mortgage.

Avoid cashback deals: Here's a rough-and-ready rule of dealing with banks: if banks offer cashback deals, they're almost always a lousy deal for the consumer. Periodically, you'll see banks competing with each other through mortgage cashback deals, where you might get as much as 7 percent of your mortgage principal in a lump-sum payment. These deals are often pitched to first-time homebuyers, who may be dazed by all of the expenses they're incurring and wondering where all of the money is going to come from. My suggestion is to find it some-place other than in a cashback mortgage.

These mortgages are generally sold with no discount, or at best with a tiny one. Net result: You have a bunch of cash with which to buy furniture or pay the movers, but your mortgage is pegged to an interest rate far higher than it otherwise would be. If you want to pay the least for your mortgage, a low rate beats getting cash back.

Another point about cashback deals is that the mortgage must be kept to the end of its negotiated term, otherwise you may have to pay back the money you received.

Ask for no frills: Have you ever used the prepayment privileges on your mortgage, which allow you to pay down the principal by 10 to 20 percent a year? Probably not. While most people like the idea of being able to pay down a big chunk of what they owe, they never actually get around to doing it. If you're in this group, ask your lender about a lower interest rate in exchange for minimal prepayment room. One major mortgage broker offers a "no-frills" mortgage option, which lets you make only a 5-percent prepayment (or increase your payments by 5 percent) and guarantees rates for only thirty days. The benefit to the borrower is a five-year mortgage with a rate about 0.15 of a point lower than the regular mortgage.

Mind the amortization period: The term *amortization* refers to the number of years it will take you to fully pay off your mortgage. Your mortgage term may be one, three, five, or whatever number of years, but the amortization period tells you how long you have to go until your payments are done. The standard practice when taking out a new mortgage is to use a twenty-five-year amortization, but there's no reason why you can't ask your lender to adjust that to, say, twenty-three or twenty years (some lenders may move only in multiples of five years). Your monthly payments will rise, but the total interest cost of your mortgage will be much lower. Don't reduce your amortization period if it will crimp your household cash flow to a point where it's painful. An extra year or two of mortgage payments, to me, is well worth the benefit of less financial stress on a daily basis.

You can also shorten your amortization period when renewing or refinancing a mortgage. Ask your lender to help you compare the payments on your existing amortization period with a shorter period.

Just say no to thirty-year mortgages (and run for your life from thirty-five-year mortgages): This point really just echoes the previous one. In early 2006, the federal agency Canada Mortgage and Housing Corp. introduced a new thirty-year amortization period for mortgages, which compares to the traditional twenty-five-year period in this country (thirty-year mortgages have been available, and popular, in the American and British markets for years). Within weeks, CMHC's private sector competitor, Genworth Financial Canada, replied with a thirty-five-year mortgage. CMHC's goal was to improve housing affordability in urban centres where home prices had risen sharply. By lengthening the amortization period, of course, a homebuyer's monthly payments are smaller.

Here are some numbers to illustrate the utility of a thirty-year mortgage: with the new thirty-year amortization, a $200,000 five-year fixed-rate mortgage at 5.1 percent would require a monthly payment of $1079.35; with a twenty-five-year amortization, the monthly payment would be $1174.62. A thirty-year amortization period also allows you to afford a more expensive home. If you can afford $1500 per month in mortgage payments and have a mortgage rate of 5.1 percent, you could buy a house worth $255,000 with a twenty-five-year amortization period, or a home worth $277,000 with a thirty-year amortization period.

The rather pricey catch: Going with a thirty-year period for the $200,000 mortgage mentioned above would cost an estimated $240,533 in total interest versus $194,379 for the twenty-five year mortgage—a difference of $46,154. Now you see why I recommend that people save for a larger down payment and go with a conventional twenty-five-year amortization period.

Choose accelerated biweekly payments: This is a no-brainer money-saving tip, and one that many people have adopted, often with the encouragement of their lender. If you pay your mortgage on a monthly basis, you make twelve payments. An accelerated biweekly plan means you make a payment every two weeks, or twenty-six in a year. This has the effect of adding a thirteenth monthly payment each year. The benefit to you, the borrower, is a substantial reduction in the amount of interest you pay over the lifetime of a mortgage.

Note: It's possible to pay on a weekly basis—I do this because I find it easy to manage regular small mortgage payments—but it has only a microscopic benefit over accelerated biweekly payments in terms of interest saved.

Increase your payments: It's common for the boilerplate in a mortgage contract to allow you to boost the dollar amount of your mortgage payments by something like 10 or 15 percent each year. If you do this, the extra amount of your payment will go straight to paying down the principal and thus reduce your interest charges.

Make lump-sum payments: Again, mortgage contracts commonly allow you to make a one-time annual payment against your principal of 10 to 20 percent. Alternatively, check with your bank to see if it offers a double-up feature, whereby you can increase your regular mortgage payment at any time by up to 100 percent, or double your regular amount. Using my bank's double-up provisions, I have paid as little as $100 to top up my regular weekly mortgage payment.

YOUR FINANCIAL PROFILE: DOUBLE-UP PAYMENTS

Online Warriors: Call up a profile of your mortgage on your bank's website and look for anything that explains how to make a prepayment or double-up payment. Ideally, you will be able to specify exactly how much extra you want to pay for one or more payments.

Half and Halfers: If you don't feel comfortable playing around with your mortgage payments online, ask your personal banker to take care of this for you. You might try sending an email or fax to confirm your instructions, just so everyone understands your wishes.

Traditionalists: Call your banker to arrange this, or stop by the bank with a written note explaining what you want done.

Be careful when breaking a mortgage: We've talked a lot in this chapter about ways to get leverage over your lender while negotiating a mortgage. However, you should realize that the lender has you down on the ground with a knee to your throat when you want to get out of a mortgage that isn't open (one you can pay off in full at any time without penalty). There's no need to go into the details of mortgage penalties, but suffice it to say that they're tough and enforced with a vigour that, according to some stories I've heard, borders on glee.

That's not to say there isn't some negotiating room when breaking a mortgage, though. A lot depends on your reasons for getting out of the loan—is it to get free and clear so you can walk away, or is it to take advantage of a big drop in interest rates since you originally took on the debt? If you want a lower rate, consider a manoeuvre called the blend and extend, in which the high rate on your old mortgage is blended with a new mortgage rate, and the term of your loan is extended beyond whatever remaining time you had left. So, if you had one year left in a five-year mortgage, you'd end up with a brand new five-year mortgage.

The rate on your blended and extended mortgage won't be quite as low as if you were starting fresh, but you're still getting a substantial benefit of lower rates without penalties.

BLEND AND EXTEND IN ACTION

Here's a simplified, rough-and-ready example from the federal Financial Consumer Agency of Canada of how a blend and extend might work:

The Details

- 12 months left on your existing five-year term (sixty months)
- interest rate on your existing mortgage is 8 percent
- current rate for a five-year term is 6 percent

The Calculation

$(A + B)/C$

$A = 8\ \% \times 12$ months, or 0.96

$B = 6\ \% \times 48$ months, or 2.88

$C = 60$ months, the new mortgage term

$(0.96 + 2.88)/60 = 6.4$ percent.

Note: The FCAC says that banks use a more complex calculation that often results in a higher blended rate.

Understand mortgage default insurance: If you take out a mortgage with a down payment of less than 25 percent—lenders call
this a high-ratio mortgage—then by law you must pay for
mortgage insurance that covers your lender in case of default.
This is a very unfair requirement for borrowers who have excellent credit ratings and great cash flow, but that's life. There are
several competitors in the mortgage insurance market, notably
the federal agency Canada Mortgage and Housing Corp. and
Genworth Financial Canada. Lenders have their own prefer-
ences about whom to deal with, but for borrowers there's
virtually no difference in terms of fees and premiums.

So, how can you save on mortgage insurance? There are two
ways, the first being to ask if either mortgage insurance
provider has any special benefits for borrowers. For example,
Genworth has in the past offered a package of discounts on
moving and home-related products called Homebuyer
Privileges. The other way to save money on mortgage insurance is to build as big a down payment as possible when
buying a home.

Mortgage insurance premiums are pegged to your loan-to-
value ratio—the more you borrow, the higher your cost. If you
buy a house with a 20-percent down payment, your premium
would be 1 percent of the value of the loan. If you had a 10-per-
cent down payment, you'd pay a premium of 2 percent. With
just 5 percent down, your premium would be 2.75 percent,
which works out to a stiff $5500 on a loan of $200,000.
Remember, this amount is typically added to your mortgage,
which means you'll pay a lot of interest on it over the years.

CHAPTER FOUR IN ACTION

- Never renew a mortgage without shopping around for a better deal.

  How you'll get better value for your dollar: With housing prices as high as they are these days, even a slightly lower interest rate on a mortgage can save you a lot of money.

- Whether you are getting a new mortgage or renewing one, call a mortgage broker to at least have something against which to compare the offer from your bank.

  How you'll get better value for your dollar: Mortgage brokers generally charge nothing for their services, which consist of matching borrowers with any number of major mortgage lenders. Rates tend to be at least as good as the best deals from the banks, and there is no need to negotiate.

- Consider a variable-rate mortgage if you have the stomach for it.

  How you'll get better value for your dollar: You'll get super-low rates in comparison to conventional fixed-rate mortgages, but you run the risk of having your borrowing costs increase when interest rates rise. If you can weather some volatility, you stand a good chance of saving money in the long term.

- Know how mortgage discounting works.

  How you'll get better value for your dollar: By getting the biggest possible discount, you will minimize the considerable interest on your mortgage and help your debt become a bit more manageable through lower payments. Look for a discount off posted rates of 1 to 1.25 percentage points for longer-term mortgages and 0.5 to 0.9 points off variable-rate mortgages.

- Don't be so obsessed with getting the lowest interest rate that you forget to look at terms such as your ability to pay down the principal of your loan and, in the case of variable-rate mortgages, your flexibility in locking in to a fixed-rate mortgage.

How you'll get better value for your dollar: Paying down your mortgage can save you thousands in interest costs and get you debt-free sooner.

Conclusion: The days of applying for a mortgage like a suppli-cant are over. You're in control, and don't forget it.

FIVE

MUTUAL FUNDS

Background briefing: I've pretty much built a career by criticizing mutual funds, but you know what? I think funds are a great investing tool for the masses; I own funds myself, and I can't imagine my registered retirement savings plan without them. Probably, you should own funds, too. They're just too useful to dismiss on the basis that many funds on the market today are a disgrace to the profession of managing money.

The most important concept you can take away from this chapter is that you must pay ongoing fees to own a mutual fund (fair enough), and that you have to pay whether your fund makes money or loses it. To repeat, the compensation received by fund companies and brokers or advisers who sell funds has nothing to do with the quality of the service rendered.

It's easy to get bogged down in dreary details with funds, so let's keep things simple and to the point. Suffice it to say that fund companies dip into the money held in their funds on an ongoing basis to cover operational costs. Care to know how much money is being scooped away? It's easy to get this information—just look at a fund's management expense ratio, or MER. The MER shows you what percentage of the money in your fund is going not to you, the investor, but to your fund company. It costs money to run a mutual fund, and no reasonable person expects otherwise. And yet, it still has to be noted that MERs are a dead weight on your fund returns. Elementary mutual fund mathematics says that a fund with a 5-percent return and a 2.5-percent MER actually grossed 7.5 percent. You'll never hear about the 7.5-percent figure because fund companies always report their returns after they've paid themselves first. More fund math: A fund with a loss of 2.0 percent and an MER of 2.5 percent actually eked out a gain of 0.5 percent before the fund company paid itself.

There are many shrewd investing minds in the fund industry, and every so often I am impressed enough by someone to buy his or her fund. But there are also some people who care only about selling more mutual funds, and thus they say utterly ridiculous things about fees not mattering when you choose funds. That, readers, is what a less couth person than myself would call a big, fat lie. Fees do matter, and this is the basis for the discussion to come.

YOUR FINANCIAL PROFILE: RESEARCHING MUTUAL FUNDS

Online Warriors: You'll have access to unbelievably good resources for researching funds. This is no exaggeration. Fifteen years ago, investment advisers didn't have the kind of data and analysis you can get for free on websites such as Globefund.com (www.globefund.com), Morningstar.ca (www.morningstar.ca), and FundLibrary.com (www.fundlibrary.com). You'll also have opportunities to buy low-cost funds, but we'll save that for a bit later in this chapter.

Half and Halfers: I'm biased because I'm an employee of *The Globe and Mail*, which is part of the same corporate family as Globefund.com, but this mutual fund website is so easy to use that even a tentative Internet user can go to town.

Traditionalists: Pick some funds you're interested in and ask a relative or friend with Internet access to print off some research for you from one of the websites mentioned above.

**FIRST THINGS FIRST: HOW TO BUY FUNDS AND PAY NOTHING
(OR ONLY A LITTLE BIT) IN SALES COMMISSIONS**

To start, let's go over the lingo that mutual fund companies and investment advisers use for the various ways to buy funds:

- **Front load:** There is an upfront purchase commission. Advisers have the discretion to sell these funds with a commission that typically ranges from zero to 5 percent. In general practice, these fees should be no higher than 1 or 2 percent.
- **Back-end load, or deferred sales charge (DSC):** You pay nothing to buy a fund, but redemption fees as high as 6 percent apply if you sell your holdings within six or seven years of purchase.
- **Zero load:** A front-load fund sold with zero commission. This is the best way for investors who use an adviser to buy funds.
- **Low load:** A deferred-sales-charge fund with a token redemption fee that falls to zero after two years, instead of the usual six years.
- **No load:** Funds sold by banks and small independent fund companies (many of them of blue-chip quality) that cost nothing to buy or sell, aside from short-term trading fees. These funds are often sold directly by the company to investors; most advisers are reluctant to sell them because they pay less in compensation than mainstream funds.

There was a time—let's call it the Dark Ages—when fund investors had to pay an egregious upfront sales commission of well over 5 percent to buy a mutual fund. Then, a bright mind came up with an idea: instead of making customers pay to buy funds, sell them for free and only levy a charge if clients redeem their holdings in the first several years after they buy. This latter sales option is called the deferred sales charge, or DSC, and it's the way that a great many, but by no means all, investment advisers sell funds today.

If an adviser tries to sell you funds on a DSC basis, just say no. While it's nice to be able to buy a fund without paying a dime in commission, your freedom is too restricted if you want to sell your funds for some reason in the first several years after buying. Typically, you might pay 6 percent to sell a DSC fund in the first year or two after you buy. Imagine selling a dead dog of a fund that lost 14 percent and having to pay a 6-percent fee as well. That's one-fifth of your investment, vaporized.

Here are the alternatives to DSC funds:

1. Small Upfront Commissions
Paying a 1-percent commission—$100 on a $10,000 investment—is better than paying nothing upfront for a DSC straitjacket. A 2-percent commission starts to get pricey, while 3 percent or higher is too much.

What's in it for your adviser and his or her firm: They get the upfront commission, of course, plus an ongoing "trailer commission" (sometimes calling a trailing commission or trailer fee) paid directly to them by the fund company.

A Quick Aside about Trailing Commissions
Many financial advisers who sell mutual funds are paid in part through an honour system that assumes that you, the client, receive good continuing service in the form of regular account updates and counsel on matters such as taxes, retirement

savings, insurance needs, and budgeting. The method of payment is a money flow called a trailing commission that is sent by fund companies directly to advisers and their firms as long as you own your funds.

Let's be clear here—it's you, Mr. and Ms. Investor, who *really* pay those trailers. A major component of the fees used to calculate the management expense ratio on mutual funds goes to advisers in the form of trailing commissions. The typical widely held Canadian equity fund has an MER of about 2.4 percent or so. Of that, roughly a full percentage point would be shared by the adviser who sold the fund and his or her firm. If you want to know about the trailers you're paying, ask your adviser. You should have had all of this explained to you when you bought your funds, but maybe you forgot. Or, get a copy of your fund company's simplified prospectus (you can download prospectuses from all fund companies on a website called Sedar at www.sedar.com) and flip to the section titled Dealer Compensation.

2. Zero-Load Mutual Funds, the Way of the Future

The load, in fund parlance, is the purchase commission. With a zero-load fund, there is no commission to buy, which is the right and proper way to invest in mutual funds. Don't worry, your adviser or investment dealer will still get paid plenty for selling a zero-load fund through those trailing commissions we just looked at.

Truth be told, zero-load funds are a variant of the front-load fund, where a percentage of the amount you invest is paid as a commission at the time of purchase. The difference is that with zero-load funds, the purchase commission has been set at, you guessed it, zero. This is an important distinction because investors can sell front-load funds at will (watch out for short-term trading fees, though) without incurring the pesky redemption fees charged by DSC funds. Zero-load funds, then, are the best of all worlds. You don't pay a commission to buy them, or to sell them. One point of clarification: Zero-load funds are different from no-load funds, which cost nothing to buy or sell and offer little or no compensation to advisers. Zero-load funds pay advisers handsomely through trailing commissions.

FINDING ZERO

Although zero-load advisers are growing in number, it can be a challenge to find them. Here are some suggestions:

- *In-branch financial planners* at Royal Bank of Canada and TD Canada Trust will create a zero-load portfolio of funds for you, including third-party funds.
- *Try word of mouth* from friends, relatives, and contacts.
- *Consult the Yellow Pages* for local advisory firms, and call to ask if anyone works on a zero-load basis. You can also check web addresses listed in Yellow Page ads to see whether firms make mention of zero load.
- *Use the search engines* offered on the websites of adviser groups such as the Financial Planners Standards Council (www.cfp-ca.org) and Advocis (www.advocis.ca).

Remember, zero-load advisers can be found at small one-person outfits, larger financial planning firms, and even big brokerage houses.

Raising the subject of zero loads with a prospective adviser can be tricky. You want the adviser to know you're savvy and vigilant about fees, but you don't want to come across as a cheapskate who expects something for nothing. One approach is to ask the adviser to explain how he or she is compensated, and then ask where zero load fits in. The response you get will be a variation of one of these themes:

- Yes, certainly we can do business this way.
- Sorry, I only sell funds with a small upfront commission of 1 or 2 percent, or with a deferred sales charge.
- I find that my clients are very happy buying DSC funds.

Some advisers will only sell funds with a zero load to clients with big accounts—say, those with assets above $100,000—while others sell zero-load funds in some circumstances and DSC funds in others. Young advisers just starting out may feel they need to receive commissions when selling funds because they have a small group of clients and therefore need to maximize their revenues.

What's in it for your adviser and his or her firm: They receive your gratitude for being offered the chance to buy funds in a cost-effective way, as well as those trailing commissions paid by the fund company.

THE DOLLARS AND SENSE OF ZERO-LOAD FUNDS

Here's a hypothetical example of the financial impact of buying funds with a front load, a deferred sales charge, and zero load. My assumption is that you're buying $20,000 of a typical mainstream equity fund. Also, the ongoing cost of owning these funds is not factored in.

Option 1: Front Load

Upfront sales commission: 2%

Immediate cost: $400 taken off your principal

Future cost: $787 in lost returns over 10 years, assuming a 7-percent average annual return.

Option 2: Back-end Load

Upfront sales commission: None

Immediate cost: None

Future cost: If you sell your holdings one to six years after you buy, a sliding scale of redemption fees might cost you as much as $1200 in the first year (based on a typical 6% charge).

Option 3: Zero Load

Upfront sales commission: None

Immediate cost: None

Future cost: None

3. Low-Load Funds

Low-load funds are not a bad compromise if you run into an adviser who won't sell on a zero-load basis, and you absolutely can't stand the idea of paying an upfront sales commission. All you have to do is hold the funds for two years to eliminate redemption fees. For mainstream investors, there's little point in buying funds if you can't hold them for two years.

What's in it for your adviser and his or her firm: They receive some of the remuneration benefits of DSC, without trapping the client.

4. No-Load Funds

Banks have been amazingly successful at selling no-load funds, which leave investors free and clear of fees to buy, sell, or switch into another fund in the same family, but many other companies do the same thing. We'll look at them in greater detail later in this chapter.

What's in it for your adviser and his or her firm: There isn't much benefit, because no-load companies often pay modest trailing commissions, or none at all. That's why advisers commonly do not sell no-load funds.

5. Funds Bought through a Discount Broker

Many people think of discount brokers as the plaything of experienced speculative investors who want to trade stocks aggressively. This is true, but discount brokers are multi-faceted. These brokers love hard-trading clients because they pay a lot of money in commissions, but middle-of-the-road investors who like mutual funds are welcomed, too. Discount brokers don't offer any advice at all—that's why they can afford to charge discount commissions to stock traders—but the compensation for fund investors is that purchase and redemption fees are usually either minimal or non-existent.

YOUR FINANCIAL PROFILE: DISCOUNT BROKERS AND FUNDS

Online Warriors: You'll have the best chance to buy and sell funds without any fees at all because online brokers tend to offer the best deals to clients who conduct all of their trading on the Internet instead of by telephone with a registered representative.

Half and Halfers: Give online fund buying a try—most brokers have made it surprisingly easy.

Traditionalists: If you place a fund order by telephone, be prepared to pay either a small percentage of your purchase as a commission or a flat fee in the neighbourhood of $40.

Discounters will be covered in depth in Chapter Seven, but here's an important tip for fund investors. If you want to buy mutual funds through a discounter, draw up a list of the funds that interest you and then call around to determine which brokers sell them and whether there are any fees to buy or sell those particular funds. You don't want to go to all the trouble of setting up a discount brokerage account, only to find that the funds you want are unavailable or available only if you pay a commission fee.

What's in it for your adviser and his or her firm: You're bypassing the adviser if use a discounter.

6. Funds Bought through a Discount Fund Dealer

A small number of investment dealers focus exclusively on mutual funds and sell them on a no-fee basis, which means you can buy or sell without purchase or redemption charges. An example is Windsor, Ontario–based Sterling Mutuals, which offers thousands of different funds to investors in Ontario, Manitoba, Alberta, and British Columbia. Sterling doesn't provide any investment advice, but its service representatives do offer basic fund information. Trades can be made by telephone, fax, or over the Internet.

The most unique discount fund dealers in the country may well be ASL Direct, which several years ago pioneered the idea of rebating mutual fund trailing commissions to investors, and Agora eClient, which has recently emulated ASL's business model while adding financial advice to the mix. You remember trailing commissions—they're paid by fund companies to the advisers and investment dealers who sell their products as compensation for ongoing service to the client in the form of investment advice and financial planning. With discount brokers and fund dealers, of course, there's no advice and no service beyond basic record keeping. So how is it that discount brokers and fund dealers deserve to receive trailing commissions? They don't, actually, but no one in the investment industry seems to care much about this issue.

ASL and Agora are paid for their services by charging clients a monthly fee starting at $25 to $30, and they also require clients to pay a small fee to make a trade. These costs are offset by trailing commission rebates that can add up to 1 percent of your holding in a typical equity fund each year. The net effect is that the return you get on your funds will be 1 percentage point better than the published return. There's no doubt that not paying trailing commissions can hugely increase your returns over time, but you'll need an account with substantial assets to offset the monthly fees.

What's in it for your adviser and his or her firm: These dealers are a competitor to advisers.

A QUICK LOOK AT SOME DISCOUNT FUND DEALERS
Sterling Mutuals
Contact: www.sterlingmutuals.com; 800–354–4956; 519–256–9730
Founded: 1996
Concept: Customers pay nothing to buy funds; Sterling makes money from the trailing commissions that mutual fund companies pay to advisers. Sterling offers no investment guidance, but it provides some tools to help ensure that your mix of funds stays true to your original asset allocation.

Sterling offers access to just about every fund company, including Phillips, Hager & North, which pays no trailing commissions. Sterling has a rule that no more than 50 percent of a client's portfolio can be in PH&N funds.

Minimum account size: None
Availability: Ontario, Manitoba, Alberta, and British Columbia
Online services: You can check your statement and make trades on Sterling's website.

Coverage through the Mutual Fund Dealers Association of Canada's Investor Protection Corp: Yes, accounts held at Sterling are covered by this compensation program for people who lose money if their fund dealer goes bust.

ING Direct Funds

Contact: www.ingdirectfunds.ca; 877–464–5678; 416–497–6204
Founded: 2003
Concept: This offshoot of the online bank ING Direct offers forty funds from a group of eight fund families, including AGF, AIM-Trimark, CI, Fidelity, Franklin Templeton, and Mackenzie. ING collects trailing commissions on the funds it offers while charging no fees to buy, sell, or switch funds. Among the available funds are such familiar names as Templeton Growth, CI Harbour, Fidelity True North, and Trimark Income Growth.

ING caters to rookie investors by offering three model portfolios for conservative, moderate, and aggressive investors, each built with funds from the same eight fund families. There's also a risk questionnaire to help you decide which portfolio is right for you.
Minimum account size: None
Availability: Newfoundland, Nova Scotia, Prince Edward Island, New Brunswick, Ontario, Saskatchewan, Alberta, and British Columbia.
Online services: You can check your account, but trades must be made by phone.
Coverage through the MFDA's Investor Protection Corp: Yes

Tradex

Contact: www.tradex.ca; 800–567–3863; 613–233–3394

Founded: Third-party fund sales began in 1999; Tradex, the mutual fund company, dates back forty-five years.

Concept: Tradex operates a small low-cost, no-load family of funds that are available only to public servants and their families, but it also offers a service for all investors who want to buy third-party funds on a no-load basis.

This is a no-frills operation, but there's some compensation in the fact that there are no fees even for registered retirement accounts (other dealers may charge as much as $125). Tradex will also absorb the cost of switching your RRSP to the company.

Minimum account size: $1000

Availability: Third-party fund sales available in Ontario and Quebec

Online services: None

Coverage through the MFDA's Investor Protection Corp: Yes

Agora eClient

Contact: www.agora-eclient.com; 866–831–4490; 416–907–9631

Founded: 2003

Concept: Instead of selling funds at no cost, Agora charges a monthly fee and then rebates the trailing commissions that are part of the management expenses in your funds. Trailing commissions on equity funds typically eat up 1 percent of your returns, while bond funds account for 0.5 percent.

Agora's basic service costs $24.95 per month (there's a $99.95 set-up fee and a $9.95 fee for each buy or sell transaction), and the company estimates than you need $50,000 or so to start reaping the benefit of the trailer rebate. The real focus at this dealer, however, is not discounted fund sales but providing advice. There are varying levels of advice, with a top-line service that offers a financial plan, an annual portfolio review, and two completed tax returns. The cost is $39.95 per month, plus 0.45 to 0.65 percent of assets. Agora says you need $70,000 in your account to make this option economical.

Minimum account size: None

Availability: Ontario

Online services: None

Coverage through the MFDA's Investor Protection Corp: Indirectly, through the fund dealer Agora uses.

ASL Direct

Contact: www.asldirect.com; 800–404–4891; 416–306–9879

Founded: 2000

Concept: ASL pioneered the idea of charging investors a monthly amount and then rebating them the trailing commissions on their funds. The monthly charge is $29.95—ASL claims the fee is tax deductible for non-registered accounts—and buy, sell, and switch transactions cost $9.95 apiece.

ASL rebates trailing commissions to clients each quarter, and it claims that investor returns can be as much as 30 percent higher as those fees compound in their accounts over the years. (Note: I have heard complaints from some clients about how long it takes for their trailing commissions to be rebated.) As with Agora, there's value in this business model only if you generate more in trailing commission rebates than you pay in monthly fee and trading charges.

Minimum account size: None, but ASL suggests you have at least $30,000 to break even on its monthly fees.

Availability: Ontario, British Columbia, and Alberta

Online services: Account access, but no trading.

Coverage through the MFDA's Investor Protection Corp: Yes.

Portfolio4less.com

Contact: www.portfolio4less.com; 866–466–4745; 604–257–4745

Founded: 2005

Concept: Portfolio4less differs from the other dealers mentioned here in that it emphasizes a series of fund portfolios it has created with a thoroughness that goes beyond even what some investment advisers provide (you can also choose your own funds, if you prefer).

Each portfolio includes seven or eight funds from a wide variety of families. You'll find extensive documentation of each portfolio option on the firm's website, including historical performance. Portfolio4less is a no-load fund dealer that makes its living from trailing commissions. It also offers financial planning services to larger accounts.

Minimum account size: $20,000

Availability: Across Canada

Online services: Account access and trading.

Coverage through the MFDA's Investor Protection Corp: No

DSC FUNDS: WHY ADVISERS LIKE THEM

While they're steadily declining in popularity, some advisers continue to steer clients into DSC funds because of the juicy commissions they pay. Remember how front-load funds require you to pay a fee of 1 to 2 percent of your investment to the adviser? With DSC funds, the adviser might make as much as 5 percent upfront. You won't be paying this 5 percent, so don't get excited. Instead, the fund company will pay the commission directly to the adviser, who thereafter receives a trailing commission that is set at half the level for front-load funds.

An adviser's preference for DSC or front/zero loads offers an interesting insight into his or her business philosophy. A DSC fund pays big money upfront and less on an ongoing basis, which suggests a short-term view. The front/zero-load adviser is making a long-term bet on you as a client, forsaking the big upfront commission for a fatter payout over time.

How to Escape DSC Funds

The idea of buying a fund that drops a fat fee on you when you try to sell is decidedly against the theme of this book. But let's say you're caught in a DSC fund. What are your escape routes?

One is the good old 10-percent rule, under which most fund companies allow clients to redeem 10 percent of their holdings in a DSC fund, or move 10 percent of their holdings into a front-load fund in the same family, at no cost. An increasing number of advisers are taking advantage of this rule, automatically moving DSC money into front-load funds for clients each year. This is fine, as long as those clients have been apprised of the fact that the adviser is benefiting financially from these transactions. The reasons go back to those trailing commissions we looked at a few pages ago. With a DSC equity fund, an adviser gets that big upfront payment from the fund company, plus trailing commissions of 0.5 percent to cover customer service. By switching a client into a front-load version of the same fund, the adviser ratchets up his or her trailers to a full 1 percent. Ka-ching!

A less attractive but still useful escape route from a substandard DSC fund is to switch into another fund within the same family. Just make sure the DSC time clock, used to calculate your redemption fees on a declining scale over six or seven years, isn't reset at zero.

NOW THAT YOU KNOW HOW TO BUY FUNDS, HOW WILL YOU DECIDE WHICH FUNDS TO CHOOSE?

This question brings us back to the matter of fees and their importance in the process of choosing funds. I'm not enough of a fee zealot to tell you that fees are everything, or even the primary factor, in fund selection. But consider this: other than fees, pretty much every criterion you or your investment adviser can use to select a mutual fund relies on the past. Let's say you want to compare two mutual funds. The only way to do this is to look at factors such as performance, volatility, consistency, and managerial acumen, all of which can be judged only by results that have already occurred.

Want to know the one forward-looking criterion for selecting mutual funds? It's fees. The stock market may go into a long decline, or a fund manager may hit a wicked slump (don't think this doesn't happen), move to a new company, or try a different investing strategy that is at odds with what you're looking for in a fund. But the fees a fund charges today are more or less what it will charge a year from now, whether the manager is making money or not. It's true that a fund's MER could rise at some future point, but that's not a real worry these days thanks to a steady downward drift in fees due to increasing competitiveness in the fund industry.

It's time for a brief course in MER-ology. Some key questions:

What, exactly, is in the MER?

MERs include three different costs borne by investors. The first is the management fee, which includes salaries to portfolio managers and analysts as well as compensation to investment advisers who sell funds (advisers share these fees with their firms). The second is operating expenses, which include things like record keeping, regulatory filings, office costs, and such. The third is GST, which is charged against the management fee and some fund operating costs. To calculate the MER for a fund, you'd add up the dollar amount of each of these three cost categories and then express the total as a percentage of the assets in the fund.

Are MERs the last word on fund costs?

Alas, no, because they don't include the fees and commissions paid by fund companies to investment dealers for trading stocks and bonds. Add up these trading expenses and the penalty on a fund's performance could range from a few hundredths of a percentage point in a buy-and-hold fund to more than a percentage point in a fund run by a manager who does a lot of buying and selling. How do you find out how much of your fund returns are being eaten up by trading costs? This information should be in the semi-annual and annual management reports on fund performance that all fund companies are required to produce. Look for the "trading expense ratio," which works just like the management expense ratio in that it expresses the total brokerage costs incurred by a fund as a percentage of its assets. Add the trading expense ratio to the management expense ratio and you've pretty much nailed the amount that you as a unitholder are sacrificing in returns.

So, can MERs be considered the definitive cost measure for funds?

Though they're not all-inclusive, MERs are the best "apples-to-apples" way to compare the cost of owning funds within the same category. Be aware that fund MERs should only be compared within the same category. It makes no sense to compare global equity funds, which tend to have among the highest MERs, to money market funds, which tend to have the lowest fees.

Are data on MERs readily available?

You bet. The Globefund.com, Morningstar.ca, and FundLibrary.com websites all contain fund profiles with MER data, as do fund company websites and printed prospectuses.

GAUGING WHETHER A FUND'S MER IS TOO HIGH

To get a sense of how high a fund MER is, compare it to that of other funds in the same category.

Fund Category	Average MER for the Category
Canadian Equity	2.82 %
U.S. Equity	2.73
Global Equity	3.00
Canadian Balanced	2.64
Canadian Bond	1.83

Is your fund one of the larger ones in its category? If so, then it should enjoy economies of scale that allow it to have a lower MER than a small fund.

Fund Category	Average MER for 10 Largest Funds in the Category
Canadian Equity	2.20 %
U.S. Equity	2.33
Global Equity	2.34
Canadian Balanced	2.34
Canadian Bond	1.44

SOURCE: GLOBEFUND.COM

Fund Fees: Are They Generally Too High?

Before we address this question, let's understand that not all fund fees end up in the pockets of fund companies. On a typical equity mutual fund, a full percentage point of the MER is accounted for by a trailing commission paid to the adviser or investment dealer who sold it.

Now, are fund fees too high? The answer is no. Truth is, fund fees are as high as investors permit them to be. If investors are oblivious to fees, as they were during the fund industry's heyday in the 1990s, then companies will pretty much charge what they want. If investors wise up about fees, as they started to do in the aftermath of the bear market that began this decade, then fund companies react.

Yes, fund companies have most definitely been lowering fees. Big names such as Fidelity and CI Funds got the ball rolling in 2005, partly in reaction to rising awareness among investors about fees and partly as an outgrowth of competition in the fund industry. Mind you, this is all trivia to the sort of savvy investor you'll be after you finish reading this book. Such an investor never worries about whether fund fees are high, low, or somewhere in between. Why? Because no matter what the broad environment is for fund fees, there are always individual funds and fund families that charge less than their competitors and offer excellent value to investors. You just have to know where to find them.

BASIC FUND FEE ARITHMETIC

Imagine that you're considering an investment in two well-regarded Canadian equity funds, one with an average cost of ownership—MER, in other words—and another with very low ownership fees. Here's an analysis of how they might stack up against each other.

Fees

Fund One has a management expense ratio of 2.55 percent

Fund Two has a management expense ratio of 1.75 percent

Assumptions

- No commissions paid to buy either fund
- Both funds make an average annual 10-percent return, before fees are applied
- Your holding period for both funds will be 10 years
- $10,000 will be invested in both funds

	Fund One After 10 Years	Fund Two After 10 Years
Total fees paid:	$ 3756.19	$ 2682.54
Lost profit potential due to fees*:	$ 1908.71	$ 1338.59
Value of your investment after fees:	$ 20,272.52	$ 21,916.30

* This refers to money that, if not paid in fees, would have been invested and thus gained value over the years.

SOURCE: THE MUTUAL FUND FEE IMPACT CALCULATOR OFFERED BY THE INVESTOR EDUCATION FUND ON ITS WEBSITE AT WWW.INVESTORED.CA.

Fund Fees in Perspective

In addition to considering a fund's MER, you should also look at such factors as its returns in both the short and the long term, the consistency of those returns (big spikes up and down make for an uncomfortable ownership experience), and the extent of a fund's losses in its worst year. Also, look at the fund's investing strategy, its management team, and its compatibility with everything else you own.

Once you've got a short list of funds, be extra skeptical about the funds with the highest MERs and extra receptive to the funds with the lowest fees. High fees do not mean that a fund is a bad investment, and low fees don't guarantee anything. But there's no getting around the fact that a frugally run fund leaves more money on the table for investors.

In any dialogue with fund industry types about fees, there comes a time when what I call the "genius factor" is raised. This refers to the belief among many people that a smart fund manager—a genius, if you will—can generate such super-duper returns for investors that the fees on his or her funds are immaterial. This, my friends, is wishful thinking in most cases. While it is true that some managers have generated bountiful returns over the years, you should expect many of them to perform about average over time and to lag behind the stock market indexes they use to benchmark their performance. There are tens of billions of dollars in these funds—maybe your retirement savings, or the money you're saving for your children's post-secondary education. What a waste.

The bottom line: Fees are an often ignored, yet vitally important factor in choosing mutual funds. Now, let's put this information to work in finding you some decent funds. Here's your game plan:

1. Find the Best Values in the Mainstream Fund World

The biggest of the big fund companies have some very good funds with reasonable fees. I stress the word *some*. Big fund companies feel the need to be all things to all investors, so they offer every possible fund and fund permutation. Net result: The quality products offered by these companies are liberally mixed with dross.

Here's a quick and easy way to find good funds at big companies: look at the largest funds by assets in a particular category (you can easily do this using the Globefund.com website). Let's take the Canadian equity category as an example. As I write this, the average management expense ratio for these funds is 2.85 percent. The largest ten funds in the group had MERs ranging from 2.76 percent to 1.85 percent, and eight were below 2.45 percent. Here are some good examples of big funds from mainstream fund families with reasonable MERs:

- *CI Canadian Investment, at 2.38 percent.* It has a long history of beating the average fund in its category, has often outperformed the S&P/TSX composite index, has survived down markets quite well, and you can buy it from almost any investment adviser with as little as $500. While 2.38 percent isn't a bargain-basement MER, in the case of this fund, it's a true value.
- *TD Canadian Equity, at 2.14 percent.* A rock-solid fund that's as accessible as your nearest TD Canada Trust branch.

- *The Trimark Fund (SC version), at 1.62 percent.* The average MER for global funds is a bloated 3.02 percent at the time of writing, so you can see what a deal this fund is. More importantly, you get performance that is vastly better than average over the long term. By the way, the SC version of this fund is sold with an upfront service charge, which can be waived by the fund seller.
- *Mackenzie Cundill Value (C version), at 2.52 percent.* The MER of this global equity fund isn't especially low, but it's reasonable when you look at its record of consistently good returns and solid returns in rough markets.
- *RBC O'Shaughnessy U.S. Value, at 1.58 percent.* This fund's MER is slightly more than a full percentage point below the category average for U.S. equity funds. Returns have crushed most competitors over most periods.

You might be wondering why the average MERs for the Canadian, global, and U.S. equity categories are much higher than those of the five funds highlighted above. The average numbers are driven up by smaller fund companies that can't make a go of it unless they charge hefty fees. Big companies can charge less, but they make more in the end because they have greater assets to apply their fees against. Don't get the idea that all big fund companies are good guys, though. You have to evaluate their funds on an individual basis to ensure, first, that the fees are reasonable and, second, that the performance is there.

How to talk to your adviser about mainstream fund fees: After you've signed on with an adviser, he or she will often present you with a recommended list of mutual funds that were selected according to your investing profile. The adviser may have picked these funds herself, or they may have been on a list of products recommended by in-house or external analysts. Any decent fund picker will consider fees among other factors, but just to be sure, it's worth asking how the MERs for the funds chosen on your behalf compare to the category average. If there are any fee hogs on the list, press your adviser to justify the choice.

2. Look at Low-Cost Funds

Remember the no-load funds highlighted earlier in this chapter, the ones that cost nothing to buy or sell? Well, they sometimes have much lower than average MERs as well. These fund families tend to sell their funds directly to investors, or through discount brokers. Investment advisers can certainly sell them, too, but most of them treat these funds like toxic waste.

The reason has to do with those trailing commissions that fund companies pay advisers to cover the cost of ongoing service to clients. Most no-load companies pay only token trailing commissions, or none at all. In other words, there's little or no financial incentive for an adviser to offer these funds to clients.

Beyond low fees and no buy or sell commissions, there is one other compelling reason to look at low-cost, no-load mutual funds. Many of the companies in this category are actually pension fund managers that offer mutual funds to retail investors on the side as a way of wringing a bit of extra value out of their operations. If you buy these funds, you also get the same shrewd gang of money managers that work on behalf of corporate pension funds, endowments, non-profit organizations, and sundry rich folks. Not all institutional money managers—that's what they call people who run pension funds—are brilliant, mind you. Still, the pension fund managers that also run mutual funds are among the best of their kind. Let's look at some examples:

- **Beutel Goodman & Co:** This company looks after assets of more than $13 billion and has been around since 1967. Value investing is stressed here, which means the emphasis is on stocks that are undervalued. Beutel offers a full range of funds, with a $10,000 minimum upfront investment. Contact: 800–461–4551; www.beutel-can.com

- **Leith Wheeler Investment Counsel:** A Vancouver money manager with about $6 billion in assets and a very small fund family, with a minimum investment of $25,000 (you can divide this amount among several funds). Contact: 888–292–1122; www.leithwheeler.com

- **Mawer Investment Management:** A Calgary-based outfit that was founded in 1974. The minimum investment is $5000. Contact: 800–889–6248; www.mawer.com

- **McLean Budden:** This firm has been looking after money for institutions and wealthy individuals since 1947. The minimum investment is $10,000. Contact: 416–862–9624; www.mcleanbudden.com

- **Phillips, Hager & North:** A Vancouver firm that has built a very large mutual fund franchise on top of its successful institutional business thanks to some of the lowest fees in the fund industry. The minimum investment is $25,000, but this amount can be divided among various funds. Contact: 800–661–6141; www.phn.com

- **Sceptre Investment Counsel:** This firm has been around since 1955 and in recent years has featured one of the top-performing Canadian equity funds, which is a bit unusual in that pension/mutual fund families tend to feature quiet, steady performers. The minimum investment is $5000. Contact: 800–265–1888; www.sceptre.ca

It's important to remember when dealing with companies like these that they don't excel at everything, which means you may not want to give them all of your money. Example: Phillips, Hager & North has struggled to deliver decent results from its U.S. and global equity funds, even while it runs among the best Canadian dividend and Canadian bond funds around. Check out PH&N Dividend Income and you'll see it has an MER of 1.16 percent, which is vastly lower than the category average of 2.5 percent. This fee advantage is a major reason why the fund has been well above average over the long term.

Other Low-Fee Fund Families of Note

- **ABC Funds:** An upfront investment of at least $150,000 buys you the services of Irwin Michael, one of the sharpest investing minds in the country and an adherent of value investing, in which overlooked and undervalued stocks are sought. Contact: 877–673–6222; www.abcfunds.com
- **Chou Associates Management:** Run by Francis Chou, one of the more accomplished and honourable people in the fund industry, this family of funds combines low fees and very strong returns over the long term in its Canadian and U.S. equity funds. Chou

emphasizes safety in his investing. The minimum investment is $10,000. Contact: 888–357–5070; www.choufunds.com

- **GBC Asset Management:** This manager of money for high-net-worth individuals offers a successful growth fund, which focuses on companies with fast-growing revenues and profits. The minimum investment is $100,000. Contact: 800–668–7383; www.gbc.ca
- **MD Funds Management:** A family of funds for people in the medical profession and their families. The fees are much lower than average, and the outside managers who run the funds are generally good. The minimum investment is $3000. Contact: 800–267–4022; www.mdm.ca
- **Saxon Mutual Funds:** Funds like Saxon Stock and Saxon World Growth are low-cost gems with many years of fine returns behind them. The minimum investment is $5000. Contact: 888–287–2966; www.saxonfunds.com

How to talk to your adviser about low-fee funds: First, it has to be said that there is a small—make that very small—minority of advisers who willingly sell low-fee, or no-load, funds to clients. If your adviser balks, it will almost certainly be because these funds don't offer the same level of remuneration as mainstream funds. One way to get around this is to pay an upfront sales commission, which might seem crazy when you consider that one of the big attractions of a no-load fund is to avoid purchase costs. Still, you have to see things from your adviser's point of view. If a low-cost fund pays negligible trailing commissions, then the adviser may not earn enough revenue from your account to pay for things like personalized financial plans and such.

3. Index Investing

Fact: There are tens of billions of dollars rotting away in mutual funds that can't seem to match the returns of the stock indexes against which their performances are benchmarked. Solution: Buy the index and forget the fund. There's a bit more theory behind index investing than this, but none of it is more compelling than this.

The fund industry, which regards indexing as pure evil, has a counter-argument that goes back to the genius theory and its contention that clever managers can outperform the index on a long-term basis. It's true, some can. Can you tell which ones? Possibly. There are a few fund managers, especially in the Canadian equity category, who have long-term numbers that exceed the S&P/TSX composite by decent margins. If you, or you and your investment adviser, think you can select index-beating funds, more power to you. Just don't forget all those billions—we're talking about retirement funds, education savings funds, and other investments people are counting on—sitting in mutual funds that by the standards of all that's decent should be shut down, closed up, and otherwise put out of their misery.

YOUR FINANCIAL PROFILE: INDEXING

Online Warriors: You were born for indexing. If you're comfortable using a discount broker to buy stocks and want to invest on your own, you'll find that you can build a portfolio of exchange-traded funds (index funds that trade like a stock) for as little as $20 per trade. If you prefer index mutual funds, then you'll be able to buy the "e-series" of index funds from Toronto-Dominion Bank's mutual funds division. These e-funds are the best deal in index funds by far (more on them shortly).

Half and Halfers and Traditionalists: You have to decide whether to go the self-directed route using a discount broker (by phone, for you traditionalists), or to enlist the help of an investment adviser who uses indexing. A growing number of advisers use indexing in their client portfolios. You'll pay more than if you set up the portfolio yourself, but the compensation is that you're getting professional advice.

Entire books have been written about indexing, focusing on the academic theory behind the strategy. A quick summary will suffice here, though:

- ***Index funds are cheap to buy:*** Banks sell them on a no-load basis, which means they cost nothing to buy. The much more attractive exchange-traded fund, an index fund that trades like a stock, costs as little as $20 to $29 to buy (the minimum commission at a discount broker).

- **Index funds are cheap to own:** The manager of an index fund buys the same stocks as his target index holds, and in the same proportion. So, if Royal Bank of Canada is the biggest stock in the S&P/TSX composite index with a 5-percent weighting, RBC is also the biggest stock in an S&P/TSX composite index fund, with an identical weighting. It's robo-investing, really, and it doesn't generate anywhere near the costs to run a regular mutual fund. Net result: The ongoing ownership fee associated with index funds—the MER, in other words—is a fraction of a regular equity fund. By the way, indexing is often called passive investing because it involves none of the stock-picking that traditional funds do. This explains why regular funds are called actively managed products.

  Remember how MERs drag down the returns that individual investors receive from their funds? With index funds, returns are reduced by a much smaller load of fees than with actively managed funds. Even if an active manager beats the index by a bit, those hefty fees could depress net returns below what the index fund offered.

- **Index funds perform:** In a hot stock market, it's very common to see index funds solidly outperform most actively managed funds. As this book is being written, the TSX is coming off a super-hot three-year stretch. Canadian equity funds averaged 16.1 percent per year over that period, while the S&P/TSX composite total return index (dividends reinvested) made 21.7 percent. Even if you lowered that 21.7 percent by a full percentage point to reflect the impact of an index fund's MER, you'd still have vastly better numbers than the average fund.

Okay, you might say, the index beat the average. What about the funds that are above average? Well, there were thirty of them, or almost 14 percent of the total. You'd have had to be a good fund picker to zero in on that select group.

In the Canadian stock market, index funds tend to outperform in hot markets and traditional funds tend to do better in down markets, although some indexers would contest this point. In any case, both styles of investing do about equally well over periods of a decade or longer. Example: The average traditional Canadian equity fund made 9.2 percent annually in the twenty years before the writing of this book, while the S&P/TSX composite made 9.6 percent. If you subtracted 0.25 of a point from this return to account for the MER of an exchange-traded fund that tracks the S&P/TSX composite, you'd have 9.35 percent, or 0.15 percent more annually than the average traditional fund.

Here, we arrive at an indexing oddity. While this strategy is arguably effective in the Canadian market, it works better in the U.S. and international markets. A comparison of U.S. equity fund returns against the S&P 500 index over the twenty years before the writing of this book found that the average fund underperformed the index (measured in Canadian dollars) by 0.8 of a percentage point. A comparison of international equity funds (everywhere but North America) against the Morgan Stanley Capital International Europe, Australasia, Far East Index over the same period showed an advantage of 3.75 percentage points for the index over the average fund in the category.

Don't get too caught up in these numbers. Even long-term returns for a mutual fund can skew wildly after a few great or terrible months. The net result is that the advantage of indexing can fleetingly appear to be weak or non-existent at certain points.

- *Index funds are tax-friendly:* Stock dividends, interest from bonds, and capital gains from stocks sold at a profit are dealt with by fund companies through what are known as distributions. If you own funds in an RRSP, this is utterly irrelevant to you. Outside of an RRSP, you may find yourself with an annual tax bill resulting from these distributions. The more buying and selling a fund does, the higher the distribution may be, and the higher the resulting tax bill.

  Index funds typically do a lot less trading than most actively managed funds because they simply mirror an index, and indexes tend to have only minor changes in most years. Net result: If you own index funds outside an RRSP, you may well pay less in taxes each year as a result of distributions.

- *Index funds are easy to use:* A good metaphor for index funds, especially the exchange-traded type, is a plastic Lego brick. Just snap a few ETFs together and you've got a nice little investment portfolio suitable for RRSPs. Snap those ETFs together in a different way and you've got a speculative, highly aggressive portfolio.

  The reason why it's so easy to build portfolios like this is that there are now more than 300 ETFs available to Canadian investors on domestic and U.S. stock exchanges, each of them offering exposure to the likes of:
  - big-name stock indexes such as the S&P 500, the S&P/TSX composite, the Nasdaq 100, and the Morgan Stanley Capital International Europe, Australasia, Far East Index.

- sector indexes covering energy, mining, and gold stocks; financials; health care; consumer staples; semiconductors; and so on.
- country indexes that allow you to invest in the stock markets of countries such as Japan, Germany, and Brazil.
- bond indexes, so you can properly diversify your stock holdings.
- gold bullion and oil, through ETFs that rise and fall with the prices of the underlying commodity.

How to talk to your adviser about indexing: Be prepared to have fund-selling advisers treat you like a dope if you try to talk about indexing. My prediction is that they'll tell you, first, that the smart managers running the mutual funds they recommend outperform the index and, second, that index funds condemn you to horrible returns during bear markets. It's true that you'll lose as much as the index during bad years for the stock market, but many traditional mutual funds are going to lose big time as well. Over the long term, indexing more than holds its own.

If you deal with an investment adviser who is licensed to sell stocks, you may find he or she is more open to the idea of indexing through exchange-traded funds. That said, you'll probably find yourself encouraged to set up a fee-based account, where you pay for the services your adviser provides through fees of about 1 to 2 percent of your assets. For that money, you should get a financial plan and portfolio designed specifically for you.

INDEX FUNDS VS. ETFS

There are two ways to put indexing to work for you: through index mutual funds and exchange-traded funds, which are ultra-low-cost index funds that trade like a stock. Which is best? ETFs, hands down. The vast majority of index funds are offered by the big banks, which tend to have reasonable fees on their fund products. Index funds are a glaring exception, though. Truth be told, they're so pricey to own that you have to question whether they're worth buying at all.

The whole point of indexing is that if you can make what the index makes and pay just a bit in fees, then you can do better than many—and, often, most—actively managed funds. The average large Canadian equity fund has a management expense ratio in the area of 2.4 percent; compare that to 0.17 percent for the most popular ETF in Canada, the iShares CDN LargeCap 60 Index Fund, and an average of 0.94 percent for Canadian index funds sold by the big banks. Now, imagine that the indexes tracked by the iShares CDN LargeCap 60 Index Fund and the bank index funds each make a 10-percent annual return, before fees. Net of fees, the bank index funds leave you with an average of 9.06 percent and the iShares fund gives you 9.83 percent. Over a period of ten years, the extra performance of the iShares fund would make you an additional $1735 on a $10,000 investment.

While index funds are a clear second-best overall, they do offer some advantages. Accessibility is one—you can buy index funds over the counter at virtually any bank branch in the country. Another advantage is that index funds reinvest dividends for you at no cost, whereas dividends paid by ETFs collect as cash in your account. To reinvest them in the same ETF, you have to pay commissions. Most importantly, index funds are available on a no-load basis, so there's no cost to buy or sell. Because ETFs are essentially stocks, you need a brokerage account to purchase them and you have to pay commissions to buy and sell. An discount broker's cost for trading up to 1000 shares of most stocks typically ranges from $20 to $30, whereas a full-service broker might charge you triple that, at least.

These commissions may sound like a deterrent to buying ETFs, but that's short-sighted thinking. As a rough rule of thumb, the cheaper management expense ratio of an ETF can nullify the purchase commission at an online broker in a single year if you invest $4000 or more. For example, consider a $4000 investment in the iShares CDN LargeCap 60 Index Fund and a Canadian equity index fund, both of which deliver a one-year return before fees of 10 percent. The iShares fund has a net return of 9.83 percent, which gives you $393; the bank index fund nets 9.06 percent, or $362. The difference is $31, enough to cover the buy commission at any discount broker. A faceoff between U.S. index funds and a comparable TSX-listed ETF called the iShares CDN S&P 500 Index Fund yields a similar result.

There is a situation where ETF purchase commissions are just too onerous, and that occurs when you want to make small periodic investments, say, monthly or quarterly. You should be able to set up a contribution plan for amounts as little as $25 to $100 a month with a bank index fund, and the cost would be zero. Multiple ETF commissions for a similar plan would quickly swamp you, by comparison.

INDEX FUNDS: A COST COMPARISON

While index funds are generally a poor value, some are more cost-competitive than others. Here's a comparative snapshot using the management expense ratios in effect as this book is being written. The idea is to show you how fees can vary between fund companies.

Fund	MER
TD Canadian Index—e version	0.31%
Altamira Precision Canadian Index	0.54
RBC Canadian Index	0.74
TD Canadian Index	0.88
CIBC Canadian Index	0.96
Scotia Canadian Index	1.00
BMO Canadian Index	1.03
National Bank Canadian Index	1.14

SOURCE: GLOBEFUND.COM

"E-funds" Get an A

Index mutual funds, especially those sold by the big banks, are of questionable value because their fees are high. A notable exception is the "e series" sold by TD Asset Management, the mutual fund arm of Toronto-Dominion Bank. Here's the deal: If you're willing to buy your funds over the Internet, either directly from TDAM or from the online broker TD Waterhouse, then you can buy a variety of index funds with fees that are substantially lower than regular index funds sold by TD itself, or any other bank.

YOUR FINANCIAL PROFILE: TD'S E-FUNDS

Online Warriors: E-funds were made for you.

Half and Halfers: If you're going to try online investing, this is a good way to start.

Traditionalists: If you have an account at TD Waterhouse, see if a fund sales representative can buy e-funds for you.

Let's say you want an index fund that lets you tap into the S&P/TSX composite index. You could buy TD Canadian Index, with a management expense ratio of 0.88 percent, or TD Canadian Index-e, with an MER of 0.31 percent. Both are no-load funds, which means no commissions or fees to buy or sell, and the minimum upfront investment for both is $1000. Let's assume that the gross return before fees for both funds is 10 percent annually over ten years. Factor in the MERs of the two funds and you're left with extra returns of almost $1280 with the e version of TD Canadian Index.

The cheapest index funds after TD's e series are offered by Altamira Investment Services, a no-load fund company that sells directly to the public. The Altamira Precision Canadian Index Fund has an MER of 0.54 percent, which is very competitive when viewed against bank index funds.

The ABCs of ETFs

It sounds like a cliché to say that ETFs have exploded in popularity, but it's a fact. Whereas a decade ago there were maybe half a dozen ETFs available to Canadian and U.S. investors, now there are more than 300. With a market capitalization of more than U.S.$59 billion—that's the total value of shares outstanding—the popular Standard & Poor's Depositary Receipt, or Spider, is larger than any blue-chip Canadian stock you can name.

Institutional investors such as pension funds use ETFs, as do an increasing number of mutual fund portfolio managers. But it's not just market pros using these securities. Do-it-yourself retail investors are discovering them, and a growing number of investment advisers are also using them to build portfolios for clients. The reason is that ETFs are one of the easiest ways for investors to get the most in returns while paying the least in fees.

The appeal of ETFs starts with the fact that they're much cheaper to operate than mutual funds. As people in the fund industry say, mutual funds are sold, not bought. That means that a fund company needs fancy marketing materials, an advertising budget, and a team of salespeople whose job it is to convince investment advisers to sell their products. On top of that, fund companies need to pay the salaries of their managers and research analysts. By comparison, ETFs are dollar-store operations. As index funds, they're cheap to run, and no sales apparatus is required because they're listed on stock exchanges and trade like stocks. In practical terms, this means that the fees investors pay to own ETFs are a fraction of what they are for most types of mutual funds.

There's an ETF listed on the American Stock Exchange that tracks the S&P 500 index—it's called the iShares S&P 500 Index Fund, and it's a competitor of the aforementioned Spider—and has a management expense ratio of 0.09 percent, which is drop-dead cheap. The average U.S. equity mutual fund available to Canadian investors has an MER of 2.73, which explains why so many funds in this category have underperformed the S&P 500 over the long term. The two ETFs that cover the broad Canadian market are the iShares CDN LargeCap 60 Index Fund, with an MER of 0.17 percent, and the iShares CDN Composite Index Fund, with an MER of 0.25 percent. By comparison, the most popular Canadian equity mutual funds have MERs averaging 2.4 percent or so.

THE COST OF OWNING ETFS VS. TRADITIONAL MUTUAL FUNDS

ETF	Sector	MER	Comparable Fund MER*
iShares CDN Large Cap 60 Index Fund	Cdn Market	0.17 %	2.65 %
iShares CDN Bond Index Fund	Cdn Bonds	0.25	1.83
iShares S&P 500 Index Fund	U.S. Market	0.09	2.73
Nasdaq-100 Index Tracking Stock	Technology	0.20	2.79
iShares CDN MSCI EAFE Index Fund	International	0.50	2.61

* based on category averages

SOURCE: GLOBEFUND.COM

Short-Term Trading: Another ETF Advantage over Funds

When you buy a mutual fund, you should almost invariably be planning a long-term commitment of, let's say, five to ten years or longer. Stock and bond market volatility being what it is, you might lose money if you invest for shorter periods of time. But what if you're speculating in a volatile sector such as gold or emerging markets and want to either lock in a quick profit or cut your losses?

Mutual funds will most certainly give you your money back, but they can extract a small early redemption fee of 1 to 3 percent if you sell within one to six months of purchase (it all depends on the fund family). These fees are designed to eliminate market timing, where an investor jumps into a fund for a day, grabs a quick profit, and then flees. Market timers are freeloaders who make their gains at the expense of buy-and-hold investors, so these early redemption fees make some sense. But what if you're a lucky speculator who held for a month or two and wants out, profits in hand? Fund companies have discretion in applying short-term trading fees, but don't count on getting a bye.

A classically volatile stock market sector is gold. If you wanted to buy in, an easy option would be a precious metals mutual fund. Now, let's say you buy in when gold is at U.S.$550 per ounce, and over a wild three-month period it surges to $700. Just for the heck of it, let's say your precious metals mutual fund has risen by an identical 27 percent and you want to sell. If you owned a particular fund, you'd run smack into a 3-percent short-term trading fee that applies to investors who sell within 180 days of buying.

Some investors may not mind losing 3 percent of their gains for no good reason, especially if they've made a killing. For those who do care about such needless waste, there are ETFs like the iShares CDN Gold Sector Index Fund, which is a vehicle for investing in gold stocks that trade on the Toronto Stock Exchange. As you'll recall, ETFs have all the attributes of stocks in that you can buy and sell them at any time during the trading day, with the only cost being your broker's sell commission. These days, that commission can be as low as $20 to $30. Another aspect of this ETF advantage is your ability to sell at a moment of your choosing, hopefully when the price of your ETF has crested. With funds, you have to content yourself with the end-of-day trading price, and even then you can only count on receiving this price if you get your sell order in before 2:30 or 3 p.m. in most cases. After that, you'll receive the closing price on the next trading day.

Yet another ETF advantage is that you can place a stop-loss order, so that your broker automatically sells your holdings when the unit price falls to a predetermined level. Mutual funds offer no comparable way to control your exit price. It's worth noting that ETFs can also be sold short, which means they're a vehicle for investors with bearish feelings about a sector.

HOW TO USE ETFS TO BUILD YOUR OWN PENSION FUND

Pension fund managers are widely considered to be among the shrewdest investing professionals, because the job of managing a pension fund is so demanding. They've got to achieve returns that are sufficient to meet the obligations the fund has to present and future workers who are drawing off their pensions, while avoiding sharp losses that can set the fund off track. In other words, they must balance risk and reward. Care to have a pension fund manager look after your registered retirement savings plan? If you have a net worth of $1 million or so, you'll have your choice of high-priced talent. If not, read on.

At the heart of a pension fund is an asset allocation model, which is a fancy way of saying a blueprint calling for varying proportions of stocks, bonds, cash, and alternative investments, which can include real estate holdings such as malls, shares in private businesses, and hedge funds (in simple terms, hedge funds are a much more aggressive version of a mutual fund). Now, if you could just get your hands on a pension fund's asset allocation formula, you could reproduce it in simple fashion by using ETFs.

Psst . . . here's the formula in use recently (all I had to do to get it was call pension consulting firm Watson Wyatt Worldwide and ask for a typical portfolio breakdown of Canadian pension plans):

- Bonds: 38 percent
- Canadian equity: 30 percent
- U.S. equity: 13 percent
- International equity: 13 percent
- Cash: 3 percent
- Alternative investments: 3 percent

With this formula in hand, let's look at some of the ETF building materials you can use.

Bonds: You have three choices here: the iShares CDN Short Bond Index Fund, the iShares CDN Bond Index Fund, and the iShares CDN Real Return Bond Index Fund. The short bond fund is the least volatile of the bunch, sort of like holding a mix of one- through five-year guaranteed investment certificates. The bond index fund is a proxy for the entire Canadian bond market, while the real-return bond fund gives you exposure to a class of bonds that offer returns in excess of the inflation rate.

Like real bonds, these ETFs rise in value when interest rates decline and lose value when rates climb. But whereas bonds mature at some point and return your initial investment to you, bond ETFs are always fluctuating according to market forces. Still, these ETFs are a good bond substitute for small investors because of the low MERs of 0.25 to 0.35 percent (the average bond mutual fund MER is 1.83 percent).

Canadian stocks: Here, you have to decide whether to buy in to the S&P/TSX 60 index or the S&P/TSX composite. If you like the idea of focusing on big blue-chip stocks, consider the iShares CDN LargeCap 60 Index Fund, which tracks the sixty biggest, most heavily traded Canadian stocks. If you prefer the larger, more diverse S&P/TSX composite, which comprises approximately 280 stocks, consider the iShares CDN Composite Index Fund. Can't decide which index to use? Indexing purists would tell you to go with the broadest index, which means the S&P/TSX composite in this case.

Just to further complicate things, it's worth pointing out that there is an ETF that tracks the TSX-listed stocks with the highest dividend yields. The iShares CDN Dividend Index Fund holds a lot of stock in banks and other financial companies, as well as utilities, pipelines, and a few industrial companies such as Magna International. For someone who wants to take a very conservative approach to owning Canadian stocks, this ETF is worth a look.

U.S. stocks: A top investing bargain is the iShares S&P 500 Index Fund, which trades on the American Stock Exchange. The MER on this fund is 0.09 percent, which is a little cheaper than the 0.12 percent charged on the better known Standard & Poor's Depositary Receipts, which are often called Spiders.

Canadian investors can easily buy either of these ETFs through a full-service or discount broker, but there's a made-in-Canada option that compares well. It's called the iShares CDN S&P 500 Index Fund, and it offers exposure to the S&P 500 with currency hedging that removes both the good and the bad effects that a fluctuating Canadian dollar can have on returns from U.S. stocks. In other words, you get the return generated by the index without distortions caused by changes in the Canada–U.S. exchange rate. The MER on this fund is 0.24 percent.

If you're an investing novice or intermediate, this is all the choice you need for exposure to the U.S. market. Otherwise, it's worth taking at least a quick look at the dozens of lesser-known options available to investors who want to buy a stock index tracking the U.S. market. Examples:

- **The Vanguard Total Stock Market Viper (VTI-Amex),** which tracks the very broad Wilshire 5000 total market index and has an ultra-low MER of 0.07 percent. This fund includes small and medium-sized companies as well as large ones.

- **The iShares Russell 2000 Index Fund (IWM-Amex),** which tracks the performance of small stocks and has an MER of 0.2 percent.

- **The iShares Dow Jones Select Dividend Index Fund (DVY-New York Stock Exchange),** which holds high-yielding American stocks and has an MER of 0.4 percent.

- **The Nasdaq-100 Tracking Stock (QQQQ-Nasdaq),** which wires you into 100 of the largest non-financial stocks listed on the Nasdaq Stock Market and has a reasonable MER of 0.2 percent.

International stocks: The obvious choice for Canadians is the iShares CDN MSCI EAFE Index Fund, which offers exposure to the Morgan Stanley Capital International Europe, Australasia, Far East (EAFE) Index or, in other words, the world beyond North America. Its MER is 0.5 percent. Note that this fund is hedged to screen out the impact of currency moves.

Dozens of other global ETFs are listed on the American and New York Stock Exchanges covering both regions—Europe and the Far East, for example—or specific countries from Australia to Taiwan to the United Kingdom. The narrower the market you invest in, the more risk you incur. That's why the MSCI EAFE index is preferable for the average investor.

Alternative investments: Real estate is the easiest type of alternative investment to access through ETFs. The vehicle of choice is the iShares CDN REIT Sector Index Fund, which comprises a selection of twelve real estate investment trusts. REITs typically own a portfolio of hotels, apartments, malls, office buildings, or retirement homes, and they're one of the most stable type of income trusts around. Income trusts, by the way, are businesses that take their profits each month or quarter and pass most or all of them to unitholders through distributions of cash. The quarterly cash payouts from the iShares REIT fund yield about 5.5 percent on an annual basis, and they provide a nice complement to any gains in the unit price.

Assembling Your Pension Fund

Here's an example of how you might go about mixing the various ETF options out there:

Bonds

8% iShares CDN Real Return Bond Index Fund
  (XRB-Toronto Stock Exchange)
10% iShares CDN Short Bond Index Fund (XSB-TSX)
20% iShares CDN Bond Index Fund (XBB-TSX)

38%

Canadian Stocks

30% iShares CDN Composite Index Fund (XIC-TSX)

U.S. Stocks

10% iShares CDN S&P 500 Index Fund (XSP-TSX)
 3% iShares Russell 2000 Index Fund
  (IWM-American Stock Exchange)

13%

International Stocks

13% iShares CDN MSCI EAFE Index Fund (XIN-TSX)

Alternative Investments

3% iShares CDN REIT Sector Index Fund (XRE-TSX)

Cash

3% in any money market fund or treasury bills

How the Do-It-Yourself Pension Fund Stacks Up

Acquisition costs: Let's say that $27 is the average commission for buying up to 1000 shares of a stock (including ETFs) at a discount broker. The do-it-yourself pension fund has seven ETFs in it, which means you would face a one-time set-up fee of $189. With a fee-based investment adviser, where you pay the equivalent of 1 or 2 percent of the assets in your account each year, the cost of buying ETFs would likely be included.

As we saw earlier in this chapter, it's reasonably easy to buy mutual funds with no purchase commissions. So, it seems that our pension fund is temporarily at a disadvantage.

Ownership costs: If you weighted the MER of each of the seven ETFs in our pension fund according to its influence in the portfolio, you'd end up with 0.31 percent, or 0.39 percent if you use a typical money market fund for your 3-percent cash weighting. Here's where the do-it-yourself pension funds starts to shine. If you use typical mainstream equity and bond funds, the comparable MER for your entire portfolio might be—let's be charitable—2 percent.

Net benefit: The Mutual Fund Fee Impact Calculator on the Investor Education Fund website (www.investored.ca) allows you to compare identical investments in two funds with different MERs. Let's use it to match our pension fund portfolio against a comparable fund portfolio. If we made $10,000 in each portfolio over ten years and assumed 7-percent returns in each before fees, the fund portfolio would leave you with $16,181 and the do-it-yourself pension fund would leave you with $18,753, which represents an extra 15.9 percent. And, yes, this comparison factors in the $189 you'd pay to buy the seven ETFs in the pension fund versus zero commissions for buying the fund portfolio.

OTHER ETF PORTFOLIOS

With so many ETFs to choose from on the various North American stock exchanges, you have an incredible—some might say overwhelming—selection of portfolio building blocks. Now for some additional examples of how to use ETFs to build a portfolio. Don't take these as blueprints to be followed exactly in your own account, but rather as models to get you thinking about your own needs.

A Portfolio to Generate Income
Bonds
  5% iShares CDN Short Bond Index Fund (XSB-TSX)
  30% iShares CDN Bond Index Fund (XBB-TSX)
  ———
  35%

Stocks

35% iShares CDN Dividend Index Fund (XDV-TSX)

15% iShares Dow Jones Select Dividend Index Fund
    (DVY-NYSE)

15% iShares CDN Income Trust Sector Index Fund (XTR-TSX)

___

65%

The point of this portfolio is to generate a steady flow of income while growing your capital. You can call this total-return investing. In a taxable account—that is, outside an RRSP or registered retirement income fund (RRIF)—you might want to taper down or eliminate altogether the bonds in this portfolio. While there are definite tax advantages to income from dividends and distributions from many income trusts, interest from bonds is taxed like regular income.

A Prudently Aggressive Portfolio

Bonds

20% iShares CDN Bond Index Fund (XBB-TSX)

 5% iShares CDN Real Return Bond Index Fund (XRB-TSX)

___

25%

Canadian Stocks

35% iShares CDN Composite Index Fund (XIC-TSX)

10% iShares CDN Income Trust Sector Index Fund (XTR-TSX)

___

45%

U.S. Stocks

10% iShares Russell 3000 Index Fund
  (IWV-American Stock Exchange)

International Stocks

15% iShares CDN MSCI EAFE Index Fund (XIN-TSX)

Alternative Investments

5% iShares Comex Gold Trust (IGT-TSX)

The 70-percent weighting in stocks is a fairly aggressive stance, suitable for younger or more risk-tolerant investors. The Russell 3000 fund offers total exposure to the U.S. market, including big, medium, and small stocks, while the iShares gold fund is a handy substitute for owning gold bullion (note that it wasn't eligible for RRSP accounts as this book was published). The market price of this latter ETF is supposed to be pegged at one-tenth of the price of gold. Feel free to substitute another speculative investment here if gold doesn't suit your needs.

A Hyper-Aggressive Portfolio

Bonds

Too conservative—forget 'em.

Canadian Stocks

40% iShares CDN Composite Index Fund (XIC-TSX)
 5% iShares CDN Materials Sector Index Fund (XMA-TSX)

———

45%

U.S. Stocks

15% iShares S&P 500 Value Index Fund (IVE-Amex)

10% iShares Russell 2000 Index Fund (IWM-Amex)

5% Nasdaq-100 Index Tracking Stock (QQQQ-Nasdaq)

5% PowerShares WilderHill Clean Energy Portfolio
(PBW-Amex)

_____

35%

International Stocks

10% iShares MSCI Emerging Markets Index Fund (EEM-Amex)

5% iShares FTSE/Xinhua China 25 Index Fund (FXI-NYSE)

_____

15%

Alternative Investments

5% iShares Comex Gold Trust (IGT-TSX)

This portfolio is a bit heavy on U.S. stocks, but that's a prime hunting ground if you want speculative content. You can get aggressive with global content by using more country-specific funds, along the lines of the iShares FTSE/Xinhua China 25 Index Fund.

BACK TO INDEXING VS. MUTUAL FUNDS

I've purposely let the pendulum in this debate swing well to the side of indexing, but now it's time to let it head back toward funds, or at least partly so. Let's do that by quickly summarizing some pitfalls of ETFs and indexing that can get in the way of you employing them to maximize your investment returns while squeezing your fees to a bare minimum:

- Index investments may well perform worse than a conservatively run mutual fund in a down market.
- You need a brokerage account for ETFs, something that is intimidating for many investors.
- Brokerage commissions can add up if you trade a lot, even if you use a discount broker.
- Many investment advisers don't do indexing, whether because they're only licensed to sell mutual funds or because they think indexing is a bad strategy.
- Some mutual funds seem to defy the odds and outperform the indexes on a long-term basis.
- There's only a thin selection of index mutual funds, while the selection of ETFs is so diverse as to be confusing.

Can't decide whether to stick with mutual funds or chuck them and move to indexing? I would advise you not to get too hung up this one-or-the-other, black-vs.-white line of thinking. Instead, consider a 50–50 compromise. Indexers and proponents of traditional mutual funds often act as if their way is the only way, and they'll bury you with statistics that "prove" their position. The truth is that there are some good arguments for doing both.

If you think about it, indexing and active management can be mutually reinforcing, rather than mutually exclusive. Believers in active management argue that a smart manager can deke around stock market upsets, thereby smoothing out the volatility you'd get in an index fund and delivering higher overall returns. But even if we assume that many fund managers can actually do this, there's still a problem. When a major stock index really takes off, many fund managers can't keep up.

Combining indexing and active management can give you the best of both strategies. When the stock markets are flying, your index funds will allow you to participate fully; when the indexes are flat or falling, a conservative actively managed fund will have the opportunity to deliver.

Will your portfolio perform better with a mix of active and passive funds? There's no way to be sure, but one thing you can bank on is that you stand to benefit psychologically from owning investments that rise and fall at different times. All in all, it's a less stressful ownership experience that might lessen the temptation to make ill-advised, knee-jerk changes in your mix of investments.

Here are some factors to consider when looking for active funds that might partner well with ETFs.

- **Down-market performance:** An index fund will generally fall as much as its underlying stock index, plus a tiny bit extra because of management fees. Ideally, then, your mutual funds should exhibit more stability at times when the indexes are falling. Some good reference years are 1998, 2001, and 2002, all of which were negative for the benchmark Canadian index. Check how a fund did in these years by using the data on Globefund.com.

- **Up-market performance:** A fund that is a good complement to an ETF will probably not do as well in a hard-driving bull market.

- **Holdings:** Some mutual funds are "closet index funds," which means that they hold pretty much the same stocks as the index. Don't partner index funds with funds like these. If you have a

mutual fund of big-blue chip stocks, consider pairing it with the
iShares CDN MidCap Index Fund, which holds medium-sized
stocks. If you have a mutual fund that holds a lot of medium- or
smaller-sized companies, consider iShares CDN LargeCap 60 Index
Fund, which strictly holds big blue-chip stock.

- **Beta:** This is a fancy term for a commonly used measure of
  volatility, or the extent to which a fund bounces around as opposed
  to delivering consistent, steady returns. Funds are compared to
  their benchmark stock index, which always has a beta of one. A
  fund with a higher beta is more volatile than the index, while a
  lower beta indicates less volatility. When partnering with the index,
  you should look for lower-beta funds. Again, you can find information on beta using the fund profiles on Globefund.com.

WHERE FUND FEES REALLY HURT:
THE MONEY MARKET FUND SCANDAL

Even a diehard mutual fund industry propagandist would con-
cede that fees are crucial when it comes to money market
funds, which many people use as a super-safe parking spot for
cash in their investment account or for savings.

Money market funds invest in short-term corporate debt
instruments, where interest rates are about as low as they get.
That's one reason why money market fund returns tend to be
modest at best (lower than the high-interest savings accounts
we looked at in Chapter Two, for example). Another reason
for the meagre returns: the incredibly high MERs in this fund
class. Globefund.com tells us that the average MER for
Canadian money market funds is 1.09 percent. As of mid-
2006, the average twelve-month return for the category was

2.1 percent. See the problem? MERs are so high that fund companies are making close to as much dough off money market funds as their customers.

Yes, there are more reasonably priced money market funds, and their returns tend to be much better than average. Take the Altamira T-Bill Fund, for example. With an MER of 0.42 percent, less than half the average of its peers, this fund has managed to rank among the best performers in its category in annual returns for eight straight years. McLean Budden Money Market, at 0.55 percent, is a similarly frugal and successful fund.

Some of the lowest MERs can be found in the premium money market funds offered by all of the big-bank fund families. These funds typically have a minimum investment of $150,000 to $250,000 and MERs of 0.3 to 0.6 percent. Performance for these funds tends to be top drawer in the Canadian money market fund category, but I'd have to question the thinking of anyone with enough spare cash to be able to meet that steep six-figure upfront minimum investment. If you're in that league financially, you're almost certainly better off having a broker buy your money market instruments directly.

So where's the scandal in money market funds? It's in the fact that investors have around $40 billion wasting away in these overpriced funds, including about $12 billion in those "premium" money market funds. Generally speaking, money market funds should be used by investors of all types only as a way station for cash in a brokerage account that will soon be deployed into funds, stocks, bonds, and such. Note: As low as money market fund returns tend to be, they're better than the interest rates that brokerage firms typically pay on cash balances held in their accounts.

As for savers, they should avoid money market funds altogether. While it was popular, and sensible, to hold savings in money funds during the high-rate days of the early 1990s, today the returns are too puny to bother. You're much better off with a high-interest savings account, both for higher returns and for greater flexibility in getting money in and out of your account.

BOND FUNDS: WHERE FUND FEES HURT ALMOST AS MUCH

You'll often hear investing snobs say that bond funds are for suckers and that sophisticated investors prefer to own bonds directly. Bond funds, if well chosen, definitely make sense for small investors, but only if their fees are well below the average level of 1.83 percent. When you consider where bond yields have been in recent years—5 percent would be an exceptional return for a ten-year Government of Canada bond through much of the early part of this decade—then giving up 1.84 percent in fees seems crazy. No wonder the vast majority of bond funds can't match the return of the Scotia Capital Universe Bond Index, the benchmark used to gauge bond market performance in Canada.

One of the best bond funds in the country is Phillips, Hager & North Bond, with an MER of 0.59 percent, or about one-third the average. With a cost advantage like this, it's no wonder the fund consistently outperforms the average return for Canadian bond funds by more than a full percentage point (that's a lot when you consider that annual bond fund returns have averaged in the 5-percent range in recent years). TD Canadian Bond has a higher but still reasonable MER of 1.07 percent, and it typically comes close to the Scotia Capital index, or even surpasses it. Low fees aren't everything in bond funds—as they are in money market funds—but they are supremely important.

CHAPTER FIVE IN ACTION

- Understand the importance of fees.

  How you'll get better value for your dollar: Mutual fund companies pay themselves out of the returns they generate, so it makes sense to look at funds that are not greedy.
- Seek out zero-load investment advisers when possible.

  How you'll get better value for your dollar: There is no cost to buying zero-load funds through an adviser, so all of your investment dollars are put to work in funds. Also, there are no redemption fees if you want to sell.
- Consider the benefits of indexing for at least part of your portfolio, and don't take an investment adviser seriously if he or she has a conniption after you mention indexing.

  How you'll get better value for your dollar: Index funds are cheap to own and, in delivering the returns of any one of many different stock or bond indexes, they tend to outperform many traditional mutual funds, especially in hot markets.
- Consider a discount broker or discount fund dealer if you're a do-it-yourself fund investor.

  How you'll get better value for your dollar: There shouldn't be any cost to buy or sell funds if you use a discount dealer, and you'll have much more latitude to include low-fee funds in your portfolio.

Conclusion: Ignorance about mutual fund fees is bliss for fund companies. Wise up to the fees you're paying to buy and own your mutual funds, and make sure you're getting good value.

SIX

INVESTMENT ADVICE

Background briefing: It's hard to say who's most at fault for the abysmal lack of understanding about how much investment advice costs, and the ways in which investors pay for it. It could be the mutual fund industry's fault for hiding compensation to advisers in the sundry ongoing ownership fees that investors pay their fund companies. It could be advisers themselves, for their sometimes devious attitude toward fees and their willingness to pretend that you can be their client and pay nothing. And, it could be the fault of investors themselves for not asking the right questions about fees, and for a naive or disingenuous willingness to pretend that working with a financial professional shouldn't cost a thing.

Financial advice could be the best investment you ever make. Forget about choosing a hot equity fund or a rising stock. If you don't have an overall financial plan, you're just mucking around in a way that may or may not get you where you want to go. A good adviser provides that plan and helps you follow it over the years to a well-funded retirement, a paid-up education savings plan for your kids, and other goals like a smooth disbursement of your assets after you die.

There's a lot of debate about whether advisers are true professionals, or whether too many of them are salespeople who could just as easily be pushing cars, vacuum cleaners, or aluminium siding. Let's give advisers the benefit of the doubt and call them pros. As such, they have a perfect right to expect a decent level of compensation. Define *decent*, you say? We'll look at percentages and dollar amounts later in this chapter, but for now let's say *decent* is an amount that rewards an adviser for his or her work on your behalf without biting so deeply into your returns that your investing goals are compromised. If you're a high-net-worth investor with a seven-figure portfolio, it might mean paying a fee equal to 0.75 to 1.0 percent of your assets per year. If you're a beginner, it might mean forgoing low-fee mutual funds in favour of funds that pay fatter commissions to advisers.

The point is, investment advice must be paid for. Here's how to get your money's worth.

FIRST, SOME BACKGROUND ON FINANCIAL ADVICE

The term *adviser* is a bit vague, so let's flesh it out. To start, there are investment advisers or investment consultants who primarily sell mutual funds. A related group comprises advisers who work for brokerage houses and sell pretty much anything. People in this group used to be called brokers, but now they're more typically known as investment advisers, or IAs. Next, we have financial planners who ideally take a broad look at your financial situation and recommend various strategies and, quite likely, specific investments. Note that these are fuzzy terms with no set definition and no predetermined list of services that will be provided.

The ideal client experience with an adviser follows a six-step process that is widely used as a standard in the financial planning business:

- *Step One:* **Assessing your present situation.** Here, the adviser looks at your income, savings, investments, and debts. Assets versus liabilities, in other words.

- *Step Two:* **Identifying goals and objectives.** This step looks at your aspirations for retirement, your plans for your children's post-secondary education, and such.

- *Step Three:* **Assessing the gap, if any, between your goals and your current situation.** This is where an adviser's expertise starts to offer value for the fees you pay. As a layperson, you may be unaware of how far away you are from your goals.

- *Step Four:* **Drafting the financial plan.** The plan is a foundation of the adviser–client relationship.

- *Step Five:* **Implementing the plan.** Here, your adviser should provide a practical, usable action plan for doing what's necessary to reach your goals.

- *Step Six:* **Reviewing the plan.** Ongoing service is the name of the game here, starting at the very least with an annual meeting.

Other jobs an adviser might do include delving into how much you're paying in taxes and whether there are any opportunities for you to lower your tax bill, whether you're properly insured, and whether you have the best possible deal on your mortgage. I know of some advisers who are willing to act as a sounding board for clients even on financial questions such as whether to buy or lease a car.

The actual level of service you get from an adviser could be both a lot worse and somewhat better than this. Sadly, I'd say the chances are good that it will be worse. The reason is that a goodly number of advisers are really just sellers of investments. Yes, they *advise* you, but only to buy the whack of mutual funds they've chosen for you, probably with about ten minutes' worth of effort. If that's all the service you get from an adviser, then you'll want to be very careful about how much you'll pay her or him (you might also want to find a new adviser). On the other hand, you'd be smart to take a more open-minded attitude toward paying an adviser who takes a broader role in guiding you financially. An adviser's time costs money, and if a fair amount of time has been spent on your behalf, then you have to be prepared to pay up.

A Quick Word about RRSPs and RESPs

Want to know the most powerful arguments for using an adviser? To make sure you have enough money to retire comfortably, and enough to send your kids to a college or university that will prepare them for a rewarding career. Should you just hand over your registered retirement savings plan and registered education savings plan to an adviser, then? The answer is no. First, you need to understand a bit about how both kinds of plans work, and about the various ways you can manage them.

A surprising number of people think an RRSP is an actual product, when in fact it's simply a generic term to describe a portfolio of investments that are tax-sheltered until such time as money is withdrawn. If you choose not to have an adviser, you can walk into a bank branch, buy some mutual funds, and have them be an RRSP. You can also deal directly with a no-load mutual fund company or run your own self-directed RRSP at a discount broker.

You may well have to pay an annual administrative fee for RRSP accounts, which can easily reach $100 or more if you use an adviser (RESP fees are usually somewhat lower). Consider these fees a fact of life, although it's worth nothing that it's possible to reduce or eliminate this cost if you use a discount broker.

If an adviser is handling your RRSP and you're happy with the service and investment results, then by all means ask him or her to take on an RESP as well. Your adviser's eyes will light up when you raise the idea of expanding your relationship. As with RRSPs, you have options if you prefer to run your own RESP. Most discount brokers offer RESP accounts for which you make your own investing decisions, and bank branches can sell you RESPs made up of mutual funds. If you go the bank route, try to double-check the funds being recommended using a website such as Globefund.com or Morningstar.ca. The banks tend to be strong in Canadian equity, dividend, balanced, and income funds, but not so great in global and U.S. equity funds.

Another RESP option is a scholarship trust, which is a pool of money managed in conservative fashion by a firm that sets rules under which beneficiary students can access the money. Scholarship trusts take a conservative approach to their investing, which will certainly appeal to some investors. Be careful with these RESPs, though. There are fees, rules, and conditions associated with them that may not be apparent when reading the sales brochures.

Generally speaking, you'll pay the least in fees and commissions with self-directed RRSPs and RESPs run through a discount broker. But there's value in doing so only if you have the investing smarts to manage your own money effectively.

———

Something to bear in mind if you use an adviser is that the client experience will vary widely from firm to firm. The variables include an adviser's own preferred way of doing business, his or her firm's requirements for ethics on one hand and revenue generation on the other, and, perhaps most importantly, how much weight you carry as a client. That's weight measured in wealth, as if you didn't know. In the world of financial advice, nothing gets an adviser's attention like a portfolio in the high six-figure range or better. High-net-worth clients like these can generate a lot of revenue for advisers and their firms, and many practitioners are only interested in this crowd.

There's also no standard way of paying an adviser. In fact, advisers themselves may be willing to work under one or more different compensation models. Let's take a look at the various options.

YOUR FINANCIAL PROFILE: DEALING WITH AN ADVISER

Online Warriors: You'll most likely enjoy online access to your account, and you'll probably want to correspond with your adviser by email a lot. If you deal with an adviser at a brokerage firm, you may find that you have online access to equity research and other goodies.

Half and Halfers: You'll probably use the online account access, which is a great convenience.

Traditionalists: Face-to-face meetings and phone calls still account for a good deal of the contact between advisers and clients.

THE THREE WAYS TO PAY FOR FINANCIAL ADVICE

1. The Commission-Based Model

Imagine that you sign on with an adviser and he or she spends a few hours working up a proposed portfolio of mutual funds built to meet your investment needs, age, risk tolerance, and such. If you go ahead and buy these funds, in one way or another you will be paying for investment advice. Although many investors never realize it—sometimes it's wilful ignorance—if you buy mutual funds through an investment adviser, you pay for the privilege. If you deal with an investment adviser at a brokerage house, then you'll pay commissions to buy and sell stocks and other products, as well as mutual funds.

Advantages of the commission-based model: It's neat and clean if you're a fund investor, in that you can often avoid paying any money out of pocket for fees (unless you buy front-load mutual funds, of course).

Disadvantages: Different funds offer different compensation plans to advisers, which means there's potential for a conflict between what works best for you and what pays the most to the adviser. Also, there's an incentive for your adviser to get you to trade stocks, funds, or whatever in order to generate fresh commissions.

DEALING WITH A COMMISSION-BASED ADVISER: HOW YOU'LL PAY

Your Portfolio

$100,000 in mainstream equity and bond funds.

Upfront Charges Paid by You

- If you buy your funds with a 1-percent front load: Your $100,000 investment is reduced by $1000.
- If you buy with a deferred sales charge: You pay zero.
- If you buy from a zero-load adviser: You pay zero.

Ongoing Charges

- Your fund returns are reduced by something in the area of 0.85 percentage points each year to pay trailer fees to your adviser for continuing service. Note: This is paid out of the various fees your fund company charges against the returns its funds make, and not directly by you.

Other Potential Costs

- Switch fees, where you move from one fund within a particular family to another.
- Redemption fees of as much as 6 percent on DSC funds sold within six or seven years of purchase.

2. The Fee-Based Model

There's a simplicity and clarity to fee-based advice that has prompted many advisers to say it's the most ethical and client-friendly way to do business. We'll look at this debatable claim shortly, but for now it must be conceded that the fee-based model is easy to understand. Clients simply pay a percentage of the assets in their account, perhaps from 2.5 percent annually at the upper end for small accounts to 0.75 percent for large accounts. The fees are billed monthly or quarterly and clients can pay directly from their investment account or registered retirement account or from their bank account. The latter option is the preferable one, by the way, because it doesn't chip away at the money you have working for you in the markets.

Advantages of the fee-based model: There's no incentive for the adviser to suggest one type of investment over another, or to flog you to make trades.

Disadvantages: You might end up paying more than you would if you paid commissions only. Also, you may find that you've committed to providing a regular stream of revenue to your adviser in return for spotty or non-existent service.

DEALING WITH A FEE-BASED ADVISER: HOW YOU'LL PAY

Your Portfolio

$100,000 in stocks, bonds, and mutual funds.

Upfront Charges

• Zero

Ongoing Charges

• 1.75 percent of the value of your account each year,
  charged quarterly.

Other Potential Costs/Savings

• Heavy trading clients may pay extra costs.
• Clients with mostly bonds in their portfolio may pay less.

Theoretical Cost in Year One

• $1750

3. The Fee-Only Model

This is my favourite method of paying for financial advice, but
I don't expect many people to share this view because of the
seemingly high out-of-pocket expense. To develop an all-
encompassing financial plan for you, fee-only advisers charge
by the hour—$100 to $400 an hour would be the range—or
sometimes charge a flat fee of $1500 to $5000, or even as much
as $8000. What I like about this way of doing business is that it
reflects a straightforward transaction in which a service is

provided by the adviser and paid for by the client. It's all about the services rendered, not the investments being sold.

Advantages of the fee-only model: Clarity.

Disadvantages: Out-of-pocket expenses, and you may have to pay additional fees and commissions when you purchase investments.

DEALING WITH A FEE-ONLY ADVISER: HOW YOU'LL PAY

Your Portfolio

Not relevant.

Upfront Charges

• Your adviser will set an hourly rate, or a flat fee.

Ongoing Charges

• Not applicable.

Theoretical Total Cost

• $5000* for a full financial plan, plus a suggested investment portfolio.

* This amount is just for the sake of example. Advisers may charge more or less than this.

FINDING THE BEST ADVISER

Selecting a financial adviser on the basis that he or she has the lowest rates is no different than buying the cheapest crash helmet. Your risk is that today's bargain is tomorrow's costly catastrophe. I suggest that instead of shopping for the cheapest advice, you find the best adviser, period, and then work out the cost of the relationship and the services to be rendered.

The process of finding a good adviser may not seem to fit into our theme of getting the best value for your investing dollar, but I'm going to spend a bit of time on the topic because I have received so many pleas over the years from people having trouble in this area.

Advisers are everywhere these days—at the local strip mall, at your bank branch, in the office building where you work—but it's going to take some legwork to find one right for you. There are two reasons for this, the first being that the adviser–client relationship is a very personal one that thrives when the two parties like and respect each other. Put another way, you'll want an adviser who is compatible with you. Second, there are many crappy advisers out there. There are stupid and/or incompetent advisers who somehow earned their credentials without absorbing anything useful, there are lazy advisers who do nothing to justify their fees, and, in the extreme minority, there are predatory advisers who see your account the same way a lion views a pork chop. Yes, there are good and bad lawyers, doctors, accountants, engineers, and such out there, but the much more stringent accreditation requirements in those professions mean you don't have to be on your guard quite as much as you do when choosing a financial adviser. An additional complication in finding the right adviser may be the size of your account. The larger your account, the wider the selection of advisers you'll have. We'll look further at the matter of account size in just a moment.

Here are some ways to find an adviser:

1. Ask friends, relatives, business associates, and other professionals, such as accountants, for recommendations. Be sure to ask why someone likes his or her adviser, what type of advice he or she receives, and how well his or her portfolio has done.
2. Try the Yellow Pages under headings such as "financial planning consultants," "investment advisory service," or "investment dealers."
3. Stop by to chat with an adviser who has an office in the mall where you shop, or in an office near where you work.
4. Ask the account representative at your bank if there are any in-branch advisers who would work with you or, if you have a large account, ask for a referral to an investment adviser at the in-house brokerage firm.
5. If you're a university graduate or member of a professional association, see if any advisory firms have signed up for an affinity program.

YOUR FINANCIAL PROFILE: FINDING AN ADVISER

Online Warriors: The Financial Planners Standards Council, administrators of the Certified Financial Planner (CFP) designation, has a web-based search engine (www.cfp-ca.org) that you can use to find an adviser. Just type in the name of your community or your postal code and you'll get a list of advisers whose names you can click on for further information on matters such as compensation, preferred area of practice, and investments sold. Also try the website of the Institute of Advanced Financial Planners, which oversees the Registered Financial Planner (R.F.P.) designation (www.iafp.ca). Advocis, an organization representing advisers, has a search engine on its website (www.advocis.ca) that allows you to specify the credentials and specialties you want in an adviser.

Half and Halfers: Yellow Pages ads for advisers increasingly include web addresses that you can look up.

Traditionalists: Try the personal approach—calling around, in other words.

Choosing an Adviser: Size Matters

One of the most important factors in deciding the best type of adviser for your account is the dollar amount you have to invest. If you have a seven- or hefty six-figure portfolio, advisers will be climbing all over each other to snag you as a client. Things get trickier when you have a smaller account, especially one under $100,000.

There's little point in approaching investment advisers at major brokerage firms if your account is less than—this is an arbitrary, ballpark estimate—$250,000. More and more, these firms are focusing the attention of their best advisers on higher-net-worth clients. You may be told that your smaller account is valued, but you'll be talking to assistants rather than the boss adviser.

Independent financial planners and in-house planners at the major banks are good places to look if you have a smaller account and are content with investing in mutual funds rather than stocks (many planners are only licensed to sell funds). If you think you'd like to invest in stocks and bonds as well as funds, there are some small investment dealers catering to the $100,000-and-up market. Another possibility if you want to deal with an adviser who can sell stocks and bonds as opposed to just mutual funds is the brokerage firm Edward Jones. With an emphasis on steady, conservative investing, Jones has built a huge North American franchise by locating its offices in suburban strip malls.

Don't forget to consider the fee-only model if you have a small account. While the lump-sum payment may appear steep, it can actually be a good value if you get a thorough plan.

What Comes Next

Compile a list of prospective advisers, and then prepare some questions that you will ask each of them in an interview process that is best done in person, but can also be carried out by phone or even email. You are essentially auditioning advisers through this process, in hopes of finding one you can work with effectively. Some suggested questions:

- **What is your accreditation?** If a prospective adviser has not successfully completed one of many possible educational programs, then walk away, because you're dealing with an amateur. Among the widely recognized designations are Certified Financial Planner (CFP), Registered Financial Planner (R.F.P.), Personal Financial Planner (PFP), Chartered Financial Analyst (CFA), Chartered Financial Consultant (CH.F.C), Chartered Life Underwriter (CLU), and Canadian Investment Manager (CIM). For a complete list of designations and what they mean, try the Financial Planners Standards Council website at www.cfp-ca.org.
- **What are your typical clients like?** You don't want to be an adviser's smallest or largest account. If you're the smallest account, you'll get the least attention; if you're the largest, you may find your adviser is out of his or her depth.
- **What services do you provide?** Simply a recommended portfolio of funds, or true financial planning as well?
- **How often will I hear from you?** A common area of unhappiness for clients is the level and frequency of contact they have with their adviser. An annual meeting and periodic phone calls or emails don't seem too much to expect.
- **What kinds of investments do you use, and how do you design client portfolios?** Here's a chance for an adviser to really strut his or her stuff. Also, you'll have a chance to find out if you're dealing with an adviser who is licensed only to sell mutual funds, or all kinds of investments.
- **Can I get some references?** This is a perfectly legitimate thing to ask for.

And now for what is arguably the most important question . . .

- *What is the cost of your services, and can I get it in writing?* An adviser's handling of this question tells you most of what you need to know about his or her level of professionalism. If you get any guff from an adviser when you pose this question, simply offer this reply: How can I judge the quality of the service I will get if I don't know exactly how much I will pay?

What You Want to Hear When an Adviser Talks about Fees

One of the biggest problems with the advisory profession is its bafflingly ambivalent attitude toward fees. On one hand, advisers will talk about the need to be fairly compensated for the services they provide clients, and about the stiff overhead costs they face in areas like running an office, keeping up with regulatory requirements, paying for errors and omission insurance, and such. On the other hand, it's far too common for advisers to talk pure, unadulterated BS when it comes to fees. Certainly, advisers are getting better at explaining how they're paid. But it seems as if there's still a fear that if fees are spoken of too explicitly, clients will scamper away like frightened chipmunks.

The quality adviser is relaxed and upfront about fees because he or she knows they're well earned through the services provided to clients. Thus a conversation about compensation is not a litany of what and how the client will pay, but rather a description of services to be rendered and the resulting cost to the recipient of those services.

Ultimately, a conversation about fees will come down to your adviser telling you that he or she uses one of the three models we just looked at: commission-based, fee-based, or fee-only. Should you simply accept what you're told by an adviser about fees? I'll answer that with another question: Do you simply accept what the car salesperson says when you ask how much a vehicle costs?

How to Discuss Costs with a Prospective Adviser

Ask all of the advisers you interview to describe their cost structure, but don't bother to initiate a broader discussion of this issue unless you think the adviser is someone you can do business with. Why get into this delicate subject unless you really have to? At the same time, do not sign up with an adviser without first coming to an agreement about costs. The last thing you need is to transfer your account or hand over a cheque to an adviser only to find you can't reach a mutually agreeable arrangement on costs. Now, here's an example of how to conduct a conversation about fees with an adviser who sells mutual funds:

> **You, the Client:** Please tell me how you charge for your services.
> **Adviser:** I only sell funds on a DSC (deferred sales charge) basis.

Understanding the adviser's point of view: Young advisers who don't have a large number of clients often prefer DSC funds because of the sizable upfront commission they pay, whereas long-time advisers with many clients tend to prefer the fatter trailing commissions that front-load funds pay (Chapter Five has the lowdown on these terms). Regardless of what type of adviser you're dealing with, you have to understand that your adviser is running a business and needs to be paid in a manner that helps that business thrive.

You: I prefer not to buy DSC funds, because I don't like the idea of having to pay a redemption fee if I want to sell a few years after I buy. What alternatives do you offer?

Adviser: If you prefer, you can buy your funds on a front-load basis, which means a commission of 2 percent upfront.

You: I've heard of some advisers selling funds on a zero-load basis, with no commission upfront and no deferred sales charge. Do you do that?

Adviser: Sometimes, but not in this case. Because I provide a variety of services for new clients that require a lot of time, I need to sell funds that pay me a sales commission.

Understanding your adviser's point of view: You may find that an adviser will sell you funds on a zero-load basis, but not at first. The reasoning is that in preparing a financial plan and portfolio for you, the adviser needs to be paid the commissions available from front-load or DSC funds. In the future, when your account has grown and no longer requires the same upfront work, your adviser may be willing to sell you funds on a zero-load basis.

You: I would prefer to pay a front load of 1 percent rather than buy DSC funds.

End result: You may end up compromising with a front load of 1 or 2 percent, but avoid paying more than that. Consider DSC funds only if you are confident in your ability to buy and hold for six-plus years, in your adviser's willingness to provide continuing service for the six or seven years you're stuck in those funds, and, finally, in your adviser's ability to choose funds that will provide good value. Remember, advisers have put many billions of dollars into junk funds.

Cost Issues for Investors Who Have a Broker
Paid through Commissions

We'll use the term *broker* here to refer to someone who works as an adviser at a full-service investment dealer, where you can buy stocks and bonds as well as mutual funds, wrap accounts (discussed later in this chapter) and such. Stock-trading commissions are determined through the use of a complex grid that factors in such things as the number of shares you're buying and the price of the shares. However, there is room for negotiation on commissions, with active traders and large accounts having the best chance of getting a break.

Bonds are a trickier matter because there is no set "commission," as with a stock. Instead, your broker's firm will select a bond in its inventory, invisibly mark up its price, and then sell it to you at a profit. This markup is a crucial matter for the investor, especially at times when interest rates are low and bond yields in general are meagre. The more you pay for a bond, the less the bond's semi-annual interest payments are worth to you.

All you really need to know about bond pricing is that when your broker quotes you a yield for a bond (an annualized return that factors in the price you paid and the interest rate, or coupon, on the bond), see if you can get a better deal by having the bond's price trimmed just a bit. To reiterate, the lower the price you pay, the higher your yield. Again, large accounts have the most leverage.

More on Fee-Based Advisers

After reading the section about talking to a commission-based adviser on the subject of costs, you may well be ready to embrace the simplicity of fee-based advice. Selling point number one for the fee-based model: all chitchat about trailers, DSCs, front loads, and stock-trading commissions is rendered unnecessary. Instead of paying according to your transactions, you'll simply pay a fee pegged as a percentage of your assets.

Some of the most upstanding members of the advisory community believe that fee-based advice is the fairest way for advisers and their clients to do business, because it removes any incentive for advisers to recommend one type of investment over another to generate superior fees and commissions. Instead, trades ideally would be recommended only when they help build or protect a client's portfolio. Also, there's no incentive for the adviser to have clients buy and sell securities simply to shake some revenue out of their accounts.

REALITY CHECK: THE TAX BENEFIT OF FEE-BASED ADVICE

It's often claimed by advisory firms that fees paid for management of assets in a non-registered account may be tax deductible. The use of the word *may* here reflects the fact that, according to the Canada Revenue Agency, fees are deductible when they relate to advice on buying and selling securities, the management of securities, or tax preparation. Fees paid for financial planning services are generally not deductible, however.

You'll often hear fee-based advisers highlight one more selling point: that they and their clients are "on the same page" in that both benefit when the investments in an account rise in value. An adviser who gets 1.5 percent of a client's assets in fees every year makes an extra $525 annually if that client's account grows to $235,000 from $200,000, while the client benefits from a tidy gain in the value of his or her portfolio.

Now, let me play devil's advocate and try to pick some holes in two of the main arguments in favour of fee-based advice.

Counter-Argument #1: Yes, you do still need to worry about fees and commissions.

Sad to say, the level of ethics in the advisory profession is not robust enough to ensure that the decks have been cleared of all fees and commissions just because you're in a fee-based account. Scoring additional commissions when you're an adviser working in a fee-based arrangement is called double-dipping, and it's against the rules. Still, it can happen.

An easy way to double-dip is to include a conventional mutual fund in a fee-based account. The mutual fund pays a trailing commission to the adviser, who also receives a regular percentage-of-assets fee. Net result: The client is paying, both directly and indirectly, two streams of income in a situation where he or she should only be paying one.

Bonds are another area of concern because commissions are built in to the price of acquiring these investments. Paying a bond commission on top of your regular account fee negates the benefits of having a fee-based account. There are two possible solutions for buying bonds in a fee-based account: ask your adviser to sell you bonds without the usual price markup, or enquire about a fee reduction for the portion of your account that is devoted to bonds. For example, the fee for managing the stocks or equity funds in your portfolio might be 1.5 percent, while the bond portion is reduced to 1 percent.

The bottom line: As you have no doubt gathered by now, invisible fees and commissions are rampant in the investment industry. So, when your fee-based adviser recommends that you buy an unfamiliar investment for your account, it's a good idea to verify that there will be no additional costs to you or compensation to your adviser beyond the regular account fee.

A Quick Aside about Mutual Funds in Fee-Based Accounts

I'm a bit of a skeptic about funds in fee-based accounts, not because of anything to do with the funds per se, but rather because they're often not cost effective in this environment. Double-dipping shouldn't be a problem, because the mutual fund industry has created a special category of mutual funds called F-class that are designed to be used in fee-based accounts. F-class funds have trailing commissions stripped out of their management expense ratios, which in simple terms means that they cost less to own because they don't pay anything to advisers on an ongoing basis for client service.

The potential cost problem arises from the possibility that your regular account fee plus the reduced MER on an F-class fund will turn out to be greater than if you simply owned the regular version of the same fund. Here's an example:

F-CLASS MUTUAL FUNDS: THE GOOD AND THE BAD

Your fee-based adviser thinks you should own the Smarter Than Everyone Canadian Equity Fund.

Regular MER for this fund:	2.37%
MER for F-class version:	1.25%
Annual cost of your fee-based account:	1.50%
Your total cost:	**2.75%—Too expensive.**

Now, let's say your fee-based account is set at 1%.

MER for F-class version:	1.25%
Annual cost of your fee-based account:	1.00%
Your total cost:	**2.25%—Cost effective.**

Funds work best in fee-based accounts when they have rock-bottom MERs to begin with. Take Phillips, Hager & North's funds, for example. PH&N Dividend Income, one of the finest mutual funds in the country, has an MER of just 1.16 percent (PH&N pays no trailing commission, so there's no need for an F-class version). If you owned this fund in a fee-based account with a charge of 1.25 percent annually, it would be cost effective in the context of the broad package of financial advice you're ideally getting.

The key thing to remember with funds in a fee-based account is not to let your total cost—regular account fee plus F-class MER—rise above what you'd pay if you owned the same fund in its regular version outside a fee-based account. If you have a conscientious adviser, this should never happen. In fact, one of the benefits of a fee-based account is that it opens the door for your adviser to buy the best low-cost funds on the market, products that advisers normally ignore.

Counter-Argument #2: You and your adviser are not necessarily on the same page.

A cynic might say that investors in fee-based accounts are like dairy cows in a barn—they're milked every few months for fees. Think of advisers as the farmer and you're a lot closer than you were before to understanding why so many financial types believe that fee-based advice is the "way of the future" (some believe this because the fee-based system is ethically more pure, but the profit motive looms large for others).

The key point here is that you, the client, are milked like clockwork. This may not be a big deal, mind you. If the farmer—I mean, the adviser—takes great care of you, then you'll be getting good value for your fees. The trouble is that some advisers don't give you the substantial and consistent service needed to justify collecting 1 to 2 percent of your assets each year.

If you're talking to an adviser about a fee-based account, raise this issue by asking what ongoing service you can expect in return for the fees you pay. Remember, some advisers are all about setting up an investment portfolio for you and doing little else. Unless you receive ongoing monitoring, regular meetings, and broader financial help in areas like retirement planning, then think hard about whether you want to be a dairy cow.

Talking about Costs with Fee-Based Advisers

Here's an example of how a conversation about costs with a fee-based adviser might go:

> **Adviser:** According to my firm's schedule of fees, and with $200,000 in your account, your annual cost would be 1.75 percent of your assets.

Understanding your adviser's point of view: Costs for fee-based accounts are set down on paper, so don't think your adviser is quoting you a number out of thin air.

> **You, the client:** Okay, fine, but I'm wondering if there are any ways to shave down that fee. I'm going to have a significant portion of my account in bonds—will that help lower the fee? And I'm thinking of bringing my spouse's account over—would having both accounts with you give us both lower fees?

End Result: You can call a few other fee-based advisers to compare rates, but having a great adviser who you like is worth paying an extra, say, 0.25 of a percentage point.

A Quick Aside about Index Investing and Fee-Based Advisers

Let's say you're the sort of investor who wants and needs an adviser, even while you're sympathetic to all the arguments in favour of index investing, which is popular with self-directed investors (you can read about indexing in Chapter Five). Can you get both advice and index investing in the same package? You can, but it may not be economical unless you have a very large account in the high six-figure or even seven-figure range.

Advisers who use indexing generally work on a fee-based system, which means you have to lop fees of 1 to 2 percent off the returns you make from your index investments. Making what the indexes yield minus one percentage point is a reasonable proposition. But subtracting two percentage points from index returns will probably cut too deeply into your net investment gains.

There are top people in the advisory profession who believe in indexing, so I keep an open mind about the value their clients receive. Still, it's a good idea if you're interviewing an adviser who uses indexing to ask for some projections of how your net returns after fees would compare to other types of investments, including traditional mutual funds.

HOW TO PAY YOUR FEE-BASED ADVISER

You may have the choice of having your quarterly or monthly fees billed from your investment or registered retirement account, or debited from your bank account. For registered accounts especially, opt for debiting from your bank account.

Having fees deducted from the pool of money in your retirement savings account can limit your potential for tax-free compounding over the years. Over the period of a decade or more, we're talking about several thousands of dollars in gains thrown away to pay fees.

More on Fee-Only Advisers

Some of the most professional financial advisers I've dealt with over the years as a personal finance columnist for *The Globe and Mail* work on a fee-only arrangement, and I think this is no coincidence. The more stature you have as an adviser, the more comfortable you are in being crystal clear about how you charge for your services. Of course, there's no clearer way to charge for financial advice than to say, "At a cost of $5000, I'm going to draft a full financial plan that will help ensure that you have enough money to retire comfortably, see to it that you save enough for your children to attend university, reduce the amount of tax you pay as much as possible, and keep your debt under control."

Why don't more advisers work this way? It's simple: clients won't let them because they're so childishly skittish about fees. Also, many advisers simply don't have the credentials, the experience, and the gravitas needed to talk about costs in an utterly transparent way.

Talking about Costs with Fee-Only Advisers

Here's how a conversation about costs with a fee-only adviser might go:

> **Adviser:** I charge $400 per hour, or a flat rate that would amount to $4000, for the kind of financial plan that you and I have been talking about.

Understanding your adviser's point of view: Rates are based on the adviser's experience, stature, and such.

You, the client: Thanks, this sounds like a good arrangement. I wonder if you could draw up an estimate for me of the various aspects and costs of the plan. That might help me see if there are any ways of possibly reducing the cost.

End result: With an estimate in hand, you have the information you need to decide whether the adviser's services will be worth the projected expense. As for comparing rates, financial advice isn't a commodity product, so don't necessarily jump on the lowest bid.

Signs You're Not Getting Good Value for the Fees Paid to Your Adviser

Poor returns: Are your investment results markedly worse over a period of at least a few years than the relevant benchmarks for measuring the performance of stocks and bonds? Have you have lost money in an account for which preservation of your capital was your top goal? Are you are in demonstrably second-rate investment products that are being outpaced by quality products? If the answer to any of these questions is yes, then you've got a problem.

A word of warning: Don't judge the quality of your returns in a simplistic way, or your adviser will dismiss you as a know-nothing amateur. Poor returns are not defined as losing money or making less than the market in a particular year. In a bear market, losing less than the major stock indexes is considered an achievement, while lagging a hot market is considered normal for a conservatively managed equity fund.

Something to think about: Nothing hardens advisers against the complaints of badly served clients like a chorus of crybaby investors complaining because they got into the stock market and lost money. To repeat, losing money over a year or even two years is not in and of itself a mark of bad service.

You never hear from your adviser: In order to *advise*, an advisor must communicate with you. And yet, some advisers are never heard from again after setting up your account, unless you count those generally useless newsletters, calendars, and such. At a minimum, you should get a yearly portfolio review, either in person or by phone, and periodic emails.

Odd fees crop up on your account statement: Every dollar that comes out of your account for fees and commissions should have been explained to you in advance in plain English. Unauthorized trading, while rare, is an egregious sign that you have a rogue adviser.

You feel you've been put in investments that are more aggressive than you wanted: Spare a moment here to consider the adviser's point of view on aggressive investing. Advisers want happy clients, and one sure way to get a happy client is to produce big investment gains. This explains why advisers sometimes take a riskier stance with clients who asked to play it safe. By the way, your risk tolerance should have been clearly spelled out in the Know Your Client (KYC) form or Investment Policy Statement (IPS) that you and your adviser filled out as a getting-to-know-you exercise when you began your working relationship.

Note as well that advisers have an incentive to shun bond

funds in favour of riskier equity funds because they pay a higher level of ongoing compensation.

You're being shunted into high-cost investments with no discernible benefit: You want a low-cost mutual fund, but your adviser insists on a wrap program (basically, a diversified portfolio in a single product). You want a guaranteed investment certificate, while your adviser just loves principal-protected notes. Wraps and PPNs were popular with investors at mid-decade, but they're also prime examples of products that are more about generating revenue for the financial industry than giving clients the right tools to invest effectively.

If you have reason to believe that the investing advice you're getting is being generated by pecuniary matters, raise the issue with your adviser. Ask what the compensation for the question-able investment is, and how it compares to similar products that were not recommended. The product that pays more to your adviser is not necessarily the wrong choice, but it does require some justification.

An excessive number of transactions are being initiated by your adviser: The jargon word to describe this problem is *churning*. Technically speaking, it means recommending unnecessary trades simply to generate revenue from your account.

BAD SERVICE VS. BAD ACTORS

You can write off a lot of problems you might have with your adviser as being due to inattentiveness, sloppiness, or other factors that can be rectified with a frank conversation. But there are some offences—churning and recommending overly aggressive investments, for example—where an adviser has committed a more serious offence and quite possibly broken securities regulations. Discuss matters like these with your adviser and, if necessary, kick the matter upstairs at your adviser's firm by contacting the branch manager. If you need to escalate the matter further, head to the compliance department.

If you're out money due to adviser malfeasance and can't get the firm to cover your losses, try the Ombudsman for Banking Services and Investments (www.obsi.ca; 888–451–4519; 416–287–2877). If your adviser works for a bank-owned firm, head to the bank's own in-house ombudsman first. An alternative avenue for resolving disputes is an arbitration plan sponsored by the Investment Dealers Association of Canada. You'll have to pay costs that can amount to a few thousand dollars to use it, but your broker must participate if you initiate proceedings.

WRAPS AND PRINCIPAL-PROTECTED NOTES:
WHERE'S THE VALUE?

Wrap programs and principal-protected notes are investment products I would never own myself, because they don't pass the value-for-money test. Wraps are a sort of portfolio-in-a-box product, whereby you get a blend of mutual funds (or a more exclusive cousin called a pooled fund) tailored to your personal needs, regular rebalancing of your portfolio to keep it in tune, and specially detailed reporting on how your account is doing. PPNs allow you the opportunity to invest in a portfolio of stocks or stock indexes, mutual funds, income trusts, or commodities with a guarantee that you'll at least get your money back at the end of a period ranging from three to ten years.

Conceptually, these two products will resonate with some investors. After all, who wouldn't be intrigued by the idea of a specially customized portfolio or the possibility of investing in speculative stocks or commodities with no risk of losing money? For the most part, though, both wraps and PPNs can be dismissed as nothing more than a highly engineered fee-extraction apparatus designed by the ever-creative financial industry. The same can be said of mutual funds, of course, but I disagree. Funds are a practical way to allow small investors access to assets such as stocks, bonds, and income trusts that they would not be able to purchase and manage effectively on their own. For these people, funds are the only thing standing between them and the meagre returns of guaranteed investment certificates.

Wraps

Wraps are pitched as being more sophisticated than funds because they often feature money managers who hold themselves aloof from the plebeian masses and only serve rich people. Some of these managers are hot stuff, and some are deadheads. Hey, isn't the same true of mutual funds? Yes, it is, which means that wraps have the potential to be nothing more than mutual funds with better PR.

There are a few different categories of wrap accounts, the first being a mutual fund wrap sold by a bank or fund company. These wraps are pitched as easy all-in-one products to unsophisticated investors who mistakenly think it's a big deal to build a balanced portfolio by mixing and matching funds from various mutual fund companies. Some fund wraps use in-house funds exclusively, while others use a selection of funds from several companies.

I did an analysis of wraps sold over the counter by the big banks not too long ago and found them to be of dubious value. One problem was an occasional, but not universal, practice of making the wrap's MER higher than the combined MERs of the underlying funds. Another problem was that the people building the wrap portfolios sometimes got cute by mixing in too many funds, or funds that duplicated each other. Convenience aside, you're often better off buying individual funds than a mutual fund wrap from both a cost and a performance point of view.

A step up from fund wrap accounts is the pooled wrap, which refers to the fact that the underlying investments are an exclusive offshoot of a mutual fund called a pooled fund. The marketing material for pooled wraps will try to make you think you're playing in a higher league, but don't take this for granted. In fact, pooled fund managers may be no better than mutual fund managers at generating consistently good returns.

A third category of wrap is the privately managed account, for which the initial buy-in amount could be at least $500,000, and probably more. In that bracket, you should be able to negotiate fees for your wrap account that are markedly lower than you'd pay if you owned more conventional investments.

If your adviser suggests a wrap, here are some questions to ask:

- What are the long- and short-term returns, and how do they compare to top mutual funds and benchmark stock and bond indexes?
- Is there a benefit to a wrap in terms of a lower management expense ratio than I would get with comparable mutual funds?
- What fees do you, the adviser, get for selling a wrap, and how do they compare with mutual funds?
- What sort of financial reporting is there on my account?
- How is my mix of investment, or asset allocation, determined and then monitored on an ongoing basis, and how is this different from what would be available with a portfolio of funds or stocks?

If you're trying to choose between mutual funds and wraps, the questions above should help you make a sound decision. But if you own individual stocks and are being pressed to sell them and move into a wrap (greater diversification will be the argument, and it's a fair one), ask your adviser to compare the fees and commissions you're paying now with those you'd pay in a wrap. For buy-and-hold investors with a portfolio of blue-chip stocks, a wrap could mean a big increase in fees. Also, be sure to check the trailing commissions paid by wraps versus funds, because there are cases where wraps are more lucrative for the adviser.

Principal-Protected Notes

Principal-protected notes are an evolution of the index-linked GIC, which banks have sold for many years as a way for risk-averse investors to get some exposure to the major stock indexes in a format that guarantees they will at least break even on maturity. Noticing a decided swing to more conservative investing after the bear market that began this decade, banks and other financial players tinkered with the index-linked GIC and came up with the principal-protected note.

PPNs are an improvement over index-linked GICs, which severely limit the amount of profit you can make in a rising stock market (that's the cost of the guarantee). PPNs can be sold prior to maturity, unlike index-linked GICs, and they may not limit your upside to the same degree. Also, PPNs offer a much larger array of stock indexes, portfolios of individual stocks, income trusts, hedge funds, and commodities to invest in. Underlying all these permutations is the same basic selling point: you have the opportunity to make money without the risk of losing money.

First, let's get something straight about the idea of only getting your money back at the end of a period of several years. While there's no doubt that this is better than losing money, it's still a rather pitiful outcome when you consider the ravages of inflation, even at today's relatively tame levels. Remember, on an after-inflation basis, getting your money back after a period of several years means actually losing money. You should also consider the lost opportunity to earn even the small gains that a basic GIC would have produced.

And yet, the idea of principal protection clearly has appeal for investors who lost big in the bear market and in some cases were still under water five years later. These people have jumped into PPNs to the tune of $7 billion at mid-decade, up from a couple hundred million a few years earlier.

I suppose an argument can be made that a PPN is a worthwhile option if you absolutely can't afford to lose money over a set period of time and are willing to gamble that exposure to various stocks, stock indexes, hedge funds, or what have you will give you a better return than a plain old GIC. But for the vast majority of investors, there's ample safety in simply owning a diversified portfolio, where stocks, bonds, and ultra-safe cash (this can include treasury bills, money market funds, or even high-interest savings accounts) mesh together into something that will deliver very good long-term results and take the edge off short-term ups and downs.

PPNs are a decidedly second-best option because of their considerable costs, which can be hard to pin down. There may well be upfront commissions to pay, and there can be redemption fees if you want to sell in the first few years after you buy. On top of that, various other invisible costs are built in that squeeze your returns. Simply put, any investment with a guarantee will extract a penalty on its returns to pay for that guarantee.

If your adviser suggests PPNs, here are some questions to ask:

- What purchase commissions must I pay?
- How easy is it to sell this PPN issue prior to maturity, and what redemption fees might there be?
- Do you, the adviser, receive trailing commissions?
- What are the tax implications if I sell early or hold to maturity?
- How would my returns differ if I invested in the underlying stocks, funds, indexes, etc. outside the PPN (in a non-guaranteed format)?

SAYING GOODBYE: HOW TO GET RID OF AN ADVISER WHO IS WASTING YOUR TIME AND MONEY

First, let's be clear that changing advisers is a hassle, and that working things out with your current adviser is preferable. If you feel you're not getting good value for the fees and commissions you're paying, then schedule a meeting in person or on the phone and raise your concerns. Be specific—maybe you haven't heard from the adviser in ages, maybe you've got what appears to be a cookie-cutter portfolio of weak-performing funds, or maybe you feel you're exposed to too much or too little risk. Then, ask your adviser to be frank about whether better service is possible.

Your adviser's reply may well be no if, say, you've got a $35,000 account and haven't contributed any new money in five years. In fact, if you're a tiny account or especially quarrelsome, your adviser might simply wish you bon voyage when you launch into your "I'm not happy" speech.

If you like the firm but not the adviser, contact the branch manager (the office supervisor) and ask to have your account switched to someone else. Explain the problem with your current adviser and be sure the new person is more open to your particular needs. And what if you want to move your account to another firm? The good news is that you don't actually have to fire your adviser in person or even on the phone. Simply find a new adviser and have him or her fill out an account transfer form. The rest of the process is standard procedure. Your current adviser and firm receive a copy of your transfer request and then authorize the move of your assets to your new firm. Switches like this happen every day in the financial business.

THE FINE POINTS OF ACCOUNT SWITCHING

You have two options in moving an account from one advisory firm to another, the first being an in-kind transfer where all stocks, bonds, funds, and so on are sent along to your new account. The other kind of move is a cash transfer, where your investments are sold off and the resulting cash value is transferred.

It's almost always advisable to have an in-kind transfer done, even if your new adviser is going to sell everything you own and rebuild. With an in-kind transfer, you can control the sale of your investments so that you realize the best possible price for your stocks and avoid any redemption fees on funds. Note that transfer forms may allow you to specify that some investments be transferred in kind and others be transferred in cash.

Unfortunately, some assets—including proprietary funds and guaranteed investment certificates—may not be transferable from one financial institution to another.

Second Opinions

Let's say that you signed on with an investment adviser because you were a complete financial know-nothing but, after a while, you've built up enough knowledge to be suspicious that you're not getting decent advice. You don't really want to change advisers, but you'd like to have someone look at your account just to make sure you're on the right track. You want a second opinion, in other words.

Good luck to you, because most advisers won't provide a second opinion. They'd be happy to take you on as a client, but they're not interested in a one-off session. Increasingly, though, there are advisers who are positioning themselves as consultants who work for hourly or flat fees and are happy to provide an opinion on your financial plan. One such adviser in the Toronto area is Warren MacKenzie, author of *A Second Opinion on Your Finances* and the *CARP Financial Planning Guide* (for the Canadian Association of Retired Persons). MacKenzie's firm is called Second Opinion Investment Risk Consultants (www.investors-2ndopinion.com), and it works on a fee-only basis. No investments are sold.

CHAPTER SIX IN ACTION

- Lay the groundwork for getting good value from an adviser by conducting a thorough search for financial help.

  How you'll get better value for your dollar: The right adviser will make you money through your investments, save you money in areas like taxes, and free up your time so you can concentrate on other things.
- Make sure you get a detailed list of all fees and commissions you'll pay from your adviser.

  How you'll get better value for your dollar: Fees are usually negotiable, which means you may have an opportunity to keep more of your money working for you in the markets.
- Monitor how your investments are doing at least once or twice a year.

  How you'll get better value for your dollar: Your investment returns are an important gauge of the value you're getting for the fees and commissions paid to your adviser.

- Insist on an annual review of your portfolio and overall financial situation.

  How you'll get better value for your dollar: Regular contact is vitally important to a productive adviser–client relationship.

Conclusion: Think about your adviser as you would a contractor you're hiring to do some major work on your home. Shop carefully to find the right person, keep an eye on them while they're doing the work, and then enjoy the fruits of their labour.

SEVEN

DO-IT-YOURSELF
INVESTING

Background briefing: Sure, you can save major dollars by investing on your own, either through a discount broker or a discount fund dealer. But if you're an investing klutz, low fees aren't going to prevent you from making a mess of things. In fact, they may exacerbate the problem of your lack of financial acumen by encouraging you to trade more than you should. If you're thinking about setting up a discount brokerage account to try to speculate on stocks and you have money you can afford to see destroyed before your very eyes, then go ahead and give stock trading a whirl. But when it comes to your registered retirement savings plan, your registered retirement income fund, or your children's registered education savings plan, it's a bad idea to learn by doing. Before you send your investment adviser packing and set up a discount brokerage account or sell your bank mutual funds, be sure you have the time, knowledge, and inclination to spend the many hours per year that are needed to run a portfolio successfully.

YOUR FINANCIAL PROFILE: USING A DISCOUNT BROKER

Online Warriors: You'll get the most from a discount broker because you'll be able to do all of your trading online, where commissions are cheapest. Also, you'll have access to stock and fund research, financial planning tools, and other features that all brokers now provide on their websites. It's no wonder, then, that discount brokers are often called online brokers.

Half and Halfers: Trading stocks online sounds intimidating, but once you try it two or three times it will become routine. Also, online security is pretty close to foolproof as long as you're careful about not disclosing your passwords, so there are no worries about the privacy of your personal information while trading or reviewing your account online. This is a roundabout way of encouraging you to do as much of your trading as possible on the Internet rather than using the phone option provided by all brokers.

Traditionalists: Expect to pay a premium of up to $14 when placing trades with a live representative on the telephone rather than on your broker's secure website. If you don't mind using an automated phone service, you'll pay commissions that are only slightly pricier than online rates. While you won't have easy access to online stock and fund research, you can try to have your brokerage fax or mail it to you.

WHY A DISCOUNT BROKER? THEY SAVE YOU MONEY, BIG TIME

You can trade 1 to 1000 shares of most stocks for $19.99 to $29 using the online order system at a discount broker, while a full-service broker might charge you triple that amount as a bare minimum and possibly 2 percent of the value of the trade (share price multiplied by the number of shares traded). As well, mutual funds frequently can be purchased with no commissions, options-trading commissions are lower, annual administration fees for RRSPs are lower, and . . . well, you get the picture. By not providing any advice whatsoever, discount brokers are able to position themselves as order-takers who offer the cheapest possible way to buy and sell investments and manage your money.

If the investing-related information in this book has taught you one thing, it should be that fees matter because they cut into your returns. Thus the potential savings from dealing with a discount broker should sound mighty tempting. Hold on a moment, though. When you invest through a discount broker, you are strictly on your own. There's no one to tell you what to buy and when to sell it. There's no one to place your orders for you and ensure that they are executed properly. If things go awry, you'll speak to whoever happens to answer the phone at your broker's call centre, and not to a person who knows you and is willing to advocate on your behalf because he or she values your business. You're on your own in a broader sense, too. You have to make sure that you're properly diversified, that you haven't taken on too much risk (or too little risk), and that you're on track to retire comfortably and sustain your savings while in retirement.

I'm not trying to scare you here, just help you decide whether the cost savings of being a self-directed investor would be a false economy in your case. Remember, advice costs more than doing it yourself, but foolish investing is costlier still.

COST COMPARISON OF SETTING UP A DIY PORTFOLIO AND AN ADVISER'S PORTFOLIO

You Want to Invest

- $100,000 in mutual funds
- $100,000 in individual stocks

The Hypothetical Cost with an Adviser Running Your Portfolio

Fund Commissions	2% of $100,000:	$ 2000
Stock Commissions	2% of principal value of the amount you're investing:	$ 2000
Your cost:		**$ 4000**

The Hypothetical Cost of a DIY Portfolio Held at a Discount Broker

Fund Commissions	Zero:	$ 0
Stock Commissions	$25 x 10 stocks:	$ 250
	Your cost:	**$ 250**

Beyond Commissions: The Hidden Value of Discount Brokers

Saving money on fees and commissions is by far the most compelling reason to use a discount broker, but there are numerous other benefits that enhance the value you get for your investing dollars. Here are five such benefits:

1. Twenty-four-hour access to your account: Just about every investment dealer, advice firm, etc. offers online account access these days, so discount brokers are nothing special in this regard. Where discount brokers add an extra level of convenience is in allowing you to enter trades even when the markets are closed so that they're executed as soon as business hours begin, or during the after-hour trading sessions available on some exchanges. Let's say it's Sunday morning at 10 a.m. and you're at the computer to do a little account maintenance on your RRSP. You decide to lighten up on your Canadian equity fund and divide the amount you sell between a global fund you already own and a bond fund you want to buy. Rather than waiting until Monday, when your schedule will be full, you take advantage of your free time and enter a sell order for some of your Canadian equity fund holdings, a buy order that will direct some of the proceeds of your Canadian fund into the global fund, and another buy order that will open a position for you in the bond fund you like.

2. Multiple ways to trade: Online trading of stocks and funds means the cheapest commissions, but what if you can't get to a computer? If there's a phone handy, you can call a live representative and place a trade. Or, you can use the automated telephone trading services that most brokers provide.

3. Flexibility: Whatever mix of investments you want, discount brokers can give you the means to assemble it in your portfolio. Mixing ETFs and mutual funds? Basic. Getting out of bond funds in favour of owning actual bonds? Easy. Setting up a ladder of bonds or guaranteed investment certificates, so that you have money coming due every year over five years? Simple. In fact, some discount brokers have a "ladder" function on their online bond order screens that expedites the process of assembling a bond ladder. The flexibility of discount brokers is a contrast to those investment advisers who are licensed only to sell mutual funds, who hate indexing and thus won't sell you ETFs, who won't buy individual stocks because your account is "too small," or who always choose higher-cost mutual funds because they pay the fattest commissions.

4. *Tools and research:* Ultimately, discount brokers are a commodity service based on executing your buy and sell transactions. Where brokers differentiate themselves is in the quality of their service, the slickness of their websites, and the range of tools and research they offer to help clients plan portfolios and choose investments. Some brokers offer advanced financial planning tools that help you decide on the right blend of stocks, bonds, and cash for your portfolio, and then get into the nitty-gritty of the proportion of your stock holdings that should be in Canada versus the U.S. and global markets. Many discount brokers provide analyst research on stocks and mutual funds, and some provide screening tools to help you seek out stocks and funds with the attributes you desire (stocks with high dividend yields, for example, or Canadian equity funds with fifteen-year compound average annual returns of 10 percent or more). Others provide guided portfolios that are assembled from a list of mutual or exchange-traded funds to meet your specific investing needs.

5. *Personal satisfaction:* Effectively running your own investments is a blast, plain and simple. The emphasis here is on the word *effectively*.

DISCOUNT BROKERS: WHO ARE THE PLAYERS?

BMO InvestorLine
www.bmoinvestorline.com; 888–776–6886
Owner: Bank of Montreal

CIBC Investor's Edge
www.investorsedge.cibc.com; 800–567–3343
Owner: Canadian Imperial Bank of Commerce

Credential Direct
www.credentialdirect.ca; 877–742–2900
Owner: Canada's credit unions

Disnat
www.disnat.com; 800–463–1887
Owner: Mouvement des caisses Desjardins

eNorthern
www.enorthern.com; 888–829–7929
Owner: Northern Financial

E*Trade Canada
www.etrade.ca; 888–872–3388
Owner: E*Trade Financial

HSBC InvestDirect
www.investdirect.hsbc.ca; 866–865–4722
Owner: HSBC Holdings PLC

National Bank Direct Brokerage
www.nbc.ca; 800–363–3511

Owner: National Bank of Canada

Qtrade Investor
www.qtrade.ca; 877–787–2330

Owner: Privately held

RBC Direct Investing
www.actiondirect.com; 800–769–2560

Owner: Royal Bank of Canada

ScotiaMcLeod Direct Investing
www.scotiamcleoddirect.com; 800–263–3430

Owner: Bank of Nova Scotia

TD Waterhouse
www.tdwaterhouse.ca; 800–465–5463

Owner: Toronto-Dominion Bank

HOW TO CHOOSE A DISCOUNT BROKER,
PART I: MINIMIZING FEES

The big banks dominate the discount brokerage business, but the quality of service from bank to bank varies considerably. Don't make the mistake of automatically signing up at the brokerage operated by your own bank. Having your bank account and discount brokerage at the same financial institution can be convenient because you'll be able to switch money back and forth easily, but there are risks. One is that your bank's discount brokerage won't have the level of service you need, and another is that you'll put yourself in a position of having to pay various fees that are avoidable elsewhere. Let's look at these fees, and how to avoid them:

Annual administration fees for registered retirement accounts: If you have less than $15,000 to $25,000 in your account, you'll find that most brokers charge fees of $40 to $100, plus GST. At the time this book is being written, the only broker without an annual RRSP administration fee is E*Trade Canada.

Paying $50 a year for an RRSP may not seem like a big deal, but on a $5000 account it's like having your investment returns reduced by one percentage point each year. That's a waste, so consider waiting to set up a discount brokerage RRSP until you have a larger account. Another option is to look at a broker offering a "starter RRSP account" that allows you to invest only in mutual funds, GICs, and bonds (no stocks). At TD Waterhouse and CIBC Investor's Edge, these accounts carry an annual RRSP administration fee of just $25, which is reasonable.

Fees for small non-registered accounts: Small accounts tend not to generate much revenue for a broker, and some firms try to discourage them. At some brokers, you have to pay $15 per quarter if your account drops below $5000 (the fee is usually waived if you also have an RRSP account at the same firm).

Inactivity fees: These are a variation on the small account fee, except that they apply if you have less than $5000 in assets *and* you don't trade any stocks, bonds, or, in some cases, mutual funds over a set period—say, six months. TD Waterhouse has a $15 per quarter inactivity fee, but it's waived if you sign up for its eServices feature, where statements and trade confirmations are viewed online rather than sent by mail.

Mutual fund purchase commissions: Many brokers have a list of funds they'll sell you with no purchase costs, and another list of funds on which you'll have to pay either a flat fee (roughly $40) or a commission charged as a percentage of the amount invested. Also, check to see if there are fees to sell funds.

HOW TO CHOOSE A DISCOUNT BROKER, PART II: TRADING COMMISSIONS

The cheapest mainstream discount broker at the time of writing was E*Trade Canada, which decided in early 2006 to bust out of a cartel-like pricing scheme used by other major brokers in which the cost range was $25 to $29. E*Trade's minimum commission for trades of up to 1000 shares is $19.99, which is a considerable savings over a broker charging $29. Is this enough savings to warrant choosing E*Trade or any other broker with commissions on the cheap side?

If you trade more than occasionally, the answer may well be yes. On twenty-five trades a year, the difference between paying $19.99 and $29 is a substantial $225.25. Now, for two qualifiers. One, be sure you like the services and amenities offered by a broker with cheap commissions. It happens that E*Trade offers a very good product overall, but the same can't necessarily be said of every broker that offers cheap rates. Second, ask yourself how much you really expect to trade.

An executive at RBC Direct Investing, Royal Bank of Canada's online broker, told me a few years ago that the firm's average client traded only five or six times a year, down from ten or eleven times annually at the peak of the tech-stock bubble in March 2000. I offer this information up strictly as an indicator that middle-of-the-road investors often don't trade that much, and thus don't need to put a lot of emphasis on rock-bottom commission fees when choosing a broker.

DIRECT-ACCESS BROKERS: FRIENDS OF THE GO-GO STOCK TRADER

Direct-access brokers are high-performance online brokers for aggressive investors who do a lot of trading. The appeal of these firms is super-fast trade execution, a commission schedule that can mean lower costs, and sophisticated market data services that regular brokers rarely offer. Some things to consider if you're interested in a direct access broker:

- You'll likely have to pay a monthly subscription fee for a market data feed.
- Registered retirement accounts are not always available.
- Bonds and mutual funds aren't typically available.

Direct-access brokers such as Trade Freedom, DisnatDirect, Interactive Brokers, and Questrade have made some inroads with aggressive traders, and this hasn't gone unnoticed by mainstream online brokers. Some, like BMO InvestorLine, E*Trade, TD Waterhouse, and RBC Direct Investing, have introduced reduced commissions for clients who make a certain number of trades per month. At RBC Direct Investing, for example, you'll pay $9.95 per trade of up to 1000 shares in the Canadian market if you make a minimum of thirty transactions per quarter.

If you're shopping for a discount broker on the basis of commissions, be sure to factor in the type of stocks you'll be trading. The most widely quoted commissions generally refer to trades of up to 1000 shares. Prices for larger orders are substantially higher, and they vary widely from broker to broker. For example, Credential Direct has charged $250 for a trade of 20,000 shares of a stock costing $2.10, whereas some other brokers charged $600.

HOW TO CHOOSE A DISCOUNT BROKER, PART III: SERVICES INCLUDING BELLS, WHISTLES, AND TOYS

Consider the types of services you want and then make sure that they're available at a particular broker before opening an account. Some examples of valuable services available from online brokers include:

- *Online bond trading:* A very simple way to add bonds to your portfolio—just browse the inventory or do a search to find the kind of bonds you're looking for, say, provincial strip bonds with a term of five years. Without online bond trading, you'll have to play stenographer as someone on the phone rattles off names, dates, and numbers.

- *Financial planning and asset allocation tools:* Discount brokerage executives tell me that their clients don't make much use of these tools, but I happen to think they're a huge benefit to self-directed investors who want to know if they're on the right track. Ideally, you'll get an indication of how much you need to put away to reach your retirement goals, and a blueprint for a diversified portfolio of stocks, bonds, and cash that is calibrated according to your risk tolerance and investment goals.

- **Analyst research on stocks and funds:** Most discount brokers are part of a bank-run family of investment companies that includes a full-service brokerage with analysts who research and rate both stocks and funds. This research is a great asset for the investor looking for help in deciding which stocks and funds to buy, or seeking a second opinion. Some brokers also offer research from independent suppliers such as Standard & Poor's.

- **Electronic services:** Some of the more advanced brokers allow you to view past transactions online, going back as far as the date you opened your account. Other helpful online services include transferring money between your brokerage account and a chequing account at any bank, opening new accounts, and archiving both account statements and trade confirmation slips.

- **Access to global markets:** It's a given that a discount broker will allow you to trade on major Canadian and U.S. exchanges, but perhaps you'd like to buy stocks listed on the Hong Kong or London stock exchanges. The Canadian discount broker with the best international market access is HSBC InvestDirect, which is unique in offering online access to the Hong Kong market.

- **Real-time account updating:** Although the wonders of the Internet allow for continuous updating of the value of the stocks in your portfolio, a few laggardly brokers have not adopted real-time account updating as of the time this book is being written. Believe me, you will not be satisfied with having the prices of the stocks and bonds you own updated only once daily after the market closes.

- **Guided portfolios:** Discount brokers are not providing advice here, simply pre-assembling portfolios of mutual funds or exchange-traded funds to simplify things for newcomers to do-it-yourself investing. As long as the methodology behind these portfolios is sound, they can be a great help.

HOW TO CHOOSE A DISCOUNT BROKER, PART IV: SPECIAL OFFERS

The discount brokerage business is very competitive, so you'll often see one or more of the various players trying to attract new business with special offers such as contests to win a vacation, free trades, or payments of cash to cover any transfer-out costs assessed by your current broker. Don't pick a broker strictly on the basis of come-ons like these, but don't dismiss these offers either, because they can save you serious money. For example, it can cost $100 to $150 to extricate your RRSP from an investment dealer so you can transfer it elsewhere, while a handful of free trades can substantially boost the net returns on the stocks you buy.

Brokers seem to make their best offers during RRSP season, so it's not a bad idea to wait until early January if you're planning to open an account. If you don't see any offers on a broker's website, call the general information line and ask if there are any bonuses for new clients. If you plan to transfer an account from another broker, be sure to enquire about whether your fees will be covered.

A quick note about the mechanics of having your new broker cover your transfer costs, or give you some free stock trades: typically, you'll have to pay the transfer costs yourself (they'll be deducted from your account) and pay for any trades you make after you set up the account. Then, in the following weeks, your broker will rebate the costs to you. Be sure to monitor your account statements to verify that you have received the payments you were promised.

USING A DISCOUNT BROKER TO BUILD YOUR WEALTH, NOT YOUR BROKER'S

The first and possibly most important principle in running your own portfolio is that making many trades sucks money out of your account and puts it into your brokerage firm's pocket. Being a speculative investor, momentum trader, day trader, or any other type of aggressive stock jock is fine as long as you've taken the time to learn how it's done. But if you're a regular investor, be judicious in your trading.

Now, don't dismiss this suggestion as mere nagging. Chances are good that when you get online and place your first few trades, you're going to enjoy yourself. Let's be honest—it's a bit of a buzz to participate in that most symbolic mechanism of the free-market system, the stock exchange, from the comfort of your home computer (or—don't tell the boss—a computer at work). Maybe you'll benefit from beginner's luck and buy a stock that quickly goes up. Maybe you'll make a few more trades that fizzle, so you'll sell your mistakes and try to find something else. Next thing you know, you've racked up a few hundred dollars in trading commissions and lost a few hundred dollars on loser stock picks.

It's not the mission of this book to explain how to invest effectively in stocks, but here are a few suggestions that will help you get the best value from your discount brokerage account:

Know the difference between market orders and limit orders: A market order means that when buying a stock you'll pay the price that sellers are asking, and when selling you'll accept the price that buyers are offering. A limit order means that you put a ceiling on the price you're willing to pay and a floor on what you'll accept as a seller. Several brokers offer cheaper commissions on market orders—generally $25, versus $29 for limit orders—while other brokers charge the same price for both kinds of orders.

On very liquid stocks—those that trade frequently and thus have a gap of only a cent or two between what buyers are bidding and sellers are asking—you can get away with a market order. But if there's a bigger spread between buyers and sellers, you should consider using a limit order, even if it's more expensive. By using a limit order, you exert some control over your buy and sell prices and thus minimize the risk that you'll have to pay a large premium over the current market price to buy a stock, or that you'll have to take a haircut when selling. You may not get a limit order executed on the terms you want, but at least you have the discretion to alter your buy or sell prices to get a trade done. With a market order, you'll get instant execution of your trade, but at a price that is out of your hands.

Beware the Canada–U.S. exchange rate: If you plan to buy American stocks, be aware that brokers make big money when converting your Canadian dollars to U.S. dollars and then back to Canadian currency. In a non-registered portfolio, you can get around this problem by using a U.S.-dollar account. As this book is being written, brokers have not yet introduced a service allowing clients to maintain U.S.-dollar balances in RRSP and RRIF accounts. This feature is in high demand now that the federal government has eliminated the foreign-content limit for registered retirement accounts and thereby opened the doors to increased investments in U.S. stocks.

Don't let your cash sit idle in your account: Brokers pay only token interest on cash balances, so avoid letting funds sit around in your account unless you have plans to deploy them in the near future. A better alternative is a money market fund—you'll get a higher rate of return, enjoy near bulletproof safety, and, typically, have no problems cashing money out any time you want to make a trade. In fact, some brokers have a feature on their stock order screens that allows you to pay for a trade by selecting "take funds from my money market or T-bill fund" from a pulldown menu of payment options. Ensure that any money market fund you buy doesn't have any early redemption penalties.

Don't get hung up on buying stocks in units of 100: It's true that stocks have traditionally been bought in "board lots" of 100, but there's nothing to stop you from buying twenty-five or fifty shares, or even just a single share. Just remember to weigh the commission you're paying against the cost of the shares and the potential gain. Paying $25 in commission to acquire fifty shares of a big bank sounds like a fair bargain to me, especially if you hold those shares for decades (you'll probably find that the bank shares will split at some point, so you'll end up with 100 shares anyway).

If you're buying blue-chip stocks in odd lots (a quantity not measured in a multiple of 100), you shouldn't have to worry about paying a price premium. If you're buying a less liquid stock, you may have to pay a bit more than the going market price to have your order filled.

Consider dividend stocks: With dividend-paying stocks, you have an opportunity to make money both on share price appreciation and from the income provided by the quarterly dividend. This is called a total return, and it's a potentially powerful generator of long-term portfolio gains if you choose the right stocks. Examples would be the big banks, insurers, and other companies that are well run and profitable enough not only to maintain their dividend through good times and bad, but also to increase the payout every year or so. Watch those stocks that raise their dividends—they're sure to rise in price, too, over the long term.

Don't forget bonds: A bond from a financially strong entity such as the federal government or most provinces is a virtual certainty to pay you interest twice a year and return your money to you at maturity. This may not sound especially exciting in a hot stock market, but when the next downturn comes you'll be glad you own some bonds (or bond funds).

Use Dividend Reinvestment Plans (DRIPs): With a DRIP, the quarterly dividends paid by a stock are collected by your broker and used to buy additional shares with no commission fees charged in most cases. You'll need a sufficiently large dividend flow to pay for at least one share, because it's generally not possible to buy fractional shares through a broker-run DRIP. By contrast, DRIPs offered directly by publicly traded companies will often allow you to buy

fractional shares and thus put all of your dividends toward buying new shares. Information about company-run DRIPs is
available through a firm's investor relations department.

**Keep your trade confirmation slips and read your monthly account
statements:** Discount brokers make mistakes, so be sure you follow what's going in your account to ensure that all information
is accurate. If a problem develops, call your broker immediately
or send an email.

SOME INVESTING IDEAS TO HELP YOU USE YOUR DISCOUNT BROKERAGE ACCOUNT EFFECTIVELY

One of the best things about using a discount broker is that you
have access to virtually any type of investment. An even better
attribute: there's no one to persuade, cajole, or otherwise influence you to choose one investment over another for reasons
that have nothing to do with what will offer the best mix of risk
and return for your portfolio. But all this choice and freedom
can be overwhelming, so much so that you might be tempted
to do something destructive like let your money sit as cash in
your account so that it earns next to nothing.

Here are some suggestions on ways to build a portfolio with
a discount brokerage in such a way that you're in a position to
truly benefit from the cost savings over a full-service broker or
mutual fund–selling investment adviser.

The $100,000 Simple and Safe Portfolio
Background: A mix of steady, bulletproof income from guaranteed investment certificates plus the potential to grow your

money over time through exposure to blue-chip Canadian companies and global markets.

- **$50,000 in guaranteed investment certificates**

Notes: Use a ladder, which in this case could mean $10,000 investments in terms of one through five years. This allows you to have money coming due every year to exploit an increase in interest rates and, similarly, you won't have to renew a huge chunk of money if rates fall. Many brokers offer GICs from a variety of issuers, including some small players with much higher rates than the banks. As long as the issuer is covered by a deposit insurance plan (Canada Deposit Insurance Corp. for banks, and provincial deposit insurance plans for credit unions), you can invest with confidence provided you don't exceed the $100,000 coverage limit for CDIC and the varying limits for credit union plans (some have unlimited coverage).

- **$25,000 in a Canadian dividend fund from a mutual fund family run by one of the big banks**

Notes: The big banks all have good dividend funds, which hold blue-chip stocks that are in solid enough financial shape to pay a quarterly dividend. Dividend funds have been consistently strong over the years and tend to weather down markets reasonably well.

- **$25,000 in a global equity fund**

Notes: Use the copious amount of fund research on websites such as Globefund.com and Morningstar.ca to choose a global equity fund, which will give you exposure to stock markets all over the world, including the United States. Most of the major fund companies have a solid global equity fund, although the bank fund families have not had much success in this category.

Cost to set up: $0

Ongoing ownership cost: Reasonable—depends on the management expense ratios of the funds you choose, but something in the area of 2.35 percent for the global and dividend fund, on average.

The $100,000 Hedge-Your-Bets Portfolio

Background: A 50–50 mix of index investments, which offer the returns of widely followed stock and bond indexes, and actively managed mutual funds, in which a manager uses his or her skill to pick the best stocks available. Followers of both indexing and active management often act as if their way is the only way, but there's an argument for using both to get a "best of both worlds" benefit.

- *$15,000 in a low-fee bond fund*

Notes: Because you're investing a substantial amount of money here, you'll have access to no-load bond funds with low management expense ratios. See Chapter Five for some suggested fund families to consider.

- *$15,000 in the iShares CDN Bond Index Fund (XBB-TSX)*

Notes: This exchange-traded fund mirrors the Scotia Capital Universe Bond Index, which is a benchmark for the Canadian bond market.

- **$20,000 in the iShares CDN Composite Index Fund (XIC-TSX)**

Notes: This ETF tracks the S&P/TSX composite index, which means you're essentially buying the benchmark Canadian stock index in one fell swoop. The MER is a very low 0.25 percent, compared to an average of about 2.4 percent for popular Canadian equity funds.

- **$20,000 in a conservative Canadian equity fund**

Notes: Choose a fund that has a proven ability to weather rough markets well so as to offset the down-market risk posed by the ETF, which will go down just as much as the index in a bad year. A conservative Canadian equity fund that acts as a good partner for the iShares CDN Composite Index Fund quite likely would tend to lag the index a bit in hot markets.

- **$10,000 in the iShares CDN S&P 500 Index Fund (XSP-TSX)**

Notes: This ETF provides hedged exposure to the S&P 500 stock index, a widely followed benchmark for large U.S. stocks. The hedging feature means you'll make what the S&P 500 makes, without any impact (positive or negative) from changes in the Canada–U.S. exchange rate.

- **$10,000 in the iShares CDN MSCI EAFE Index Fund (XIN-TSX)**

Notes: Here, you get hedged exposure to the Morgan Stanley Capital International Europe, Australasia, Far East Index, which covers markets outside North America. By matching it with the S&P 500 ETF, you get global coverage with the exception of Canada.

- *$10,000 in an unhedged global equity fund*

Notes: Most global funds aren't hedged, so you shouldn't have any trouble on this count. You want an unhedged fund specifically to allow some of your portfolio to benefit if the Canadian dollar loses value against other world currencies. At the same time, of course, you're vulnerable to a rise in the Canadian dollar.

Cost to set up: $80 to $116 for the ETFs, depending on which discount broker you choose

Ongoing ownership cost: The blended MERs of the ETFs (very low cost) and the mutual funds (higher cost) would certainly be lower than if you owned a portfolio of funds sold by an investment adviser.

The $100,000 Blue-Chip Stock Portfolio

- *$25,000 in shares of the Big Five banks*

Notes: Try putting $5000 down on shares of each of the five largest banks (Bank of Montreal, Bank of Nova Scotia, Canadian Imperial Bank of Commerce, Royal Bank of Canada, and Toronto-Dominion Bank). You could try to pick a few of the best-regarded banks of the moment, but the truth is that all banks have their good and bad cycles. What unites them is a matchless reliability in not only paying their dividends each quarter, but also raising them regularly. Rising dividends will fuel your portfolio over the years, with no money lost to pay the management fees that a dividend fund would charge.

- **$10,000 in a major non-bank financial company**

Notes: You can look at insurers, fund companies, or a holding company such as Power Financial, which owns an interest in several different financial concerns. Again, rising dividends will bolster your future returns.

- **$10,000 in shares of two major utilities or pipeline companies**

Notes: Consider stocks such as Atco, Canadian Utilities, Enbridge, and TransCanada Corp., which have a record of periodically raising their dividends. They won't have as high a yield as some of their competitors, but they'll deliver higher total returns over the years (dividends plus share price appreciation).

- **$10,000 in one or two consumer staples companies**

Notes: Grocers such as Loblaws are good places to be when the stock markets hit a rough patch. Other solid dividend-paying names include cheese maker Saputo Inc. and Shoppers Drug Mart.

- **$10,000 in a consumer discretionary stock or two**

Notes: Blue-chip dividend payers to consider in this sector include Magna International and Thomson Corp.

- **$10,000 in one or two industrial stocks**

Notes: Take a look at the railroads: Canadian Pacific and Canadian National.

- **$10,000 in a telecom stock**

Notes: BCE offers a higher yield, but Telus has a better recent history of share price gains.

- *$7,500 in a mining stock or two*

Notes: There are meagre dividends here, but buy these for the sake of diversification.

- *$7,500 in an energy stock or two*

Notes: Ditto.

CHAPTER SEVEN IN ACTION

- Consider a discount broker if you have the time and, most importantly, the knowledge to run your own investment portfolio.

  How you'll get better value for your dollar: Stocks and mutual funds are much cheaper to buy and own through a discounter than through an investment adviser, which means you'll keep more of your assets working for you.
- Choose a discounter not because it's affiliated with the bank you use, but because it offers a range of investments and pricing that suit you.

  How you'll get better value for your dollar: Discount brokers differ a fair amount on their commissions and services, and you can easily end up paying more and getting less in service if you don't choose carefully.
- Trade online whenever possible.

  How you'll get better value for your dollar: Almost any transaction you can make with an online broker costs less when it's done online instead of on the telephone with a trader.
- Keep a lid on your stock trading.

  How you'll get better value for your dollar: Haphazard trading is a direct transfer of wealth from you to your broker.

Conclusion: Everything the mainstream investor needs to be successful is available from a discount broker. All that these investors need to bring to the table are the knowledge and time to look after their money.

CONCLUSION

YOU'RE A VERY BUSY PERSON, THE SERVICE YOU GET FROM your bank, broker, financial adviser, or fund company seems okay, and your family finances seem healthy enough. Do you really need to worry about whether you're getting the most in financial services for the least amount in fees, commissions, interest, and such?

Let me answer that by asking a few more questions:

- Would you like to generate a bigger return on your savings?
- Would you like to spend a little less each month on those annoying bank service fees?
- Would you like the extra cash flow you get when you pay less interest on your debts?
- Would you like the comfort of knowing that you're paying the lowest possible mortgage rate?
- Would you like to have an opportunity to increase the returns in your registered retirement savings account by paying less to a fund company or financial adviser?
- Would you like to hear about the cost savings of do-it-yourself investing?

Unless you're comatose, the answer to at least one or two of these questions has to be yes. So, let me propose a plan to get you started on the path to getting the most in financial services for the least amount of money.

Focus first on your borrowings. Carrying debt is a natural part of managing one's finances these days, but sloppy use of credit means you're transferring your wealth to a big financial company. So tally up the ways you borrow, find out the interest rates you're paying, and then refer back to Chapter Three to see if there's any way you can manage your borrowings more effectively and thus pay less in interest.

Next, tackle your banking. If you're not generating a decent rate of interest on your savings, then get to work on setting up a high-rate savings account. I fail to understand why every living bank customer in Canada doesn't already have one of these. Your next job is to look at what you're paying on a monthly basis in service fees. Everyone has their own tolerance level for service fees, but if your monthly costs are much more than $13, you should definitely read Chapter Two to see if there are any opportunities to pay less (almost certainly there are).

Ensuring that you've got the best possible mortgage is a task best suited for times when you're either looking for a new mortgage or renewing an existing one. Don't wait until a week before your renewal date to start thinking about this. Instead, mark a date three months in advance of your mortgage renewal on your calendar, and then take a look at Chapter Four for a mortgage refresher.

For many people, the hardest job of all is scrutinizing their investments, including their registered retirement savings plans and registered education savings funds. Ease into the task by grabbing as many of your monthly or quarterly account statements as you can find and tracking how you've been doing over the last while. If the stock markets have been good, have you received your fair share? If the markets have been down, are your investments hanging in, or are they being crushed? Talk to your investment adviser if any issues arise or, if you're a self-directed investor, make a detailed assessment of how your portfolio is doing against the relevant financial market benchmarks. For a guide on how to proceed, Chapters Five and Six await.

One thing I've noticed over the years about personal finance is that it's one of the few remaining areas of human activity where people are willing to bow to complexity and simply trust experts to do what's best for them. Many of these experts, I'm sad to tell you, are mainly interested in making themselves rich. We could talk for hours about how unfortunate this situation is, or you can simply take things in hand and ensure that you're paying the least and getting the most. That's what this book is all about.

ACKNOWLEDGEMENTS

Thanks to the people who read my column in *The Globe and Mail* and both educate and test me with their questions and comments. Thanks as well to the many good people in the financial industry who have helped me through the years. Two of them deserve to be singled out for their assistance with this book: Warren Baldwin of TE Financial Consultants, a true professional in the field of financial advice; and Paul Mims, veteran big-bank mortgage executive and a straight shooter.

ABOUT THE AUTHOR

As the personal finance columnist for *The Globe and Mail*, Rob Carrick is one of Canada's most trusted and widely read financial experts. He is the author of two previous books.